New Series April/May 1994
Volume 34 / Numbers 1 & 2
Edited by Alan Ross
Deputy Editor: Jeremy Lewis

London Magazine

Contents

Cover: From a drawing by Paul Emsley, Redfern Gallery.

Subscriptions £28.50 ($67) p.a. to *London Magazine*, 30 Thurloe Place, SW7. Subscription renewals, etc: Bailey Brothers, 127 Sandgate Road, Folkestone, Kent. Contributions must be accompanied by a stamped addressed envelope or International Reply Coupons. Advertising: 589 0618. We acknowledge the financial assistance of the Arts Council. Bookshop Distribution by Central Books, 99 Wallis Road E9 5LN.

© *London Magazine* 1994.

Printed by Shenval Ltd of Harlow

The Bezoar

As I read Vernell's name out loud from the student index at the back of *Irene* I felt a rush. My hand went to my pocket bezoar, and fingering its rough surface I relaxed. It still had the power to calm after all these years, this anodyne from the bowels of a wild Persian goat. The stone found its way into Dr Trigg's collection – which included examples from the chamois of Europe, the guanaco of the Andes, plus scores and scores of others – then came to me from Vernell, who said it was a prophylactic against the carnal kiss of a succubus and a proven cure for melancholia.

'Take it, Penrod. You'll need it someday.'

The bezoar isn't a topic in most high school physiology classes, though it was in ours. Coach Smiley – assigned to teach about bones, organs, muscles – wasn't really into physiology. So he had students give reports on related topics to ease his load a bit. I took Borogove to class one day and talked about vocal mechanisms in parrots. On another day Vernell brought the bezoars of her veterinarian father's collection and presented a natural history of the medicinal and mystical uses for that ancient amulet.

As she spoke, her words transported me, brought heat to my face. I was intrigued by the lore of such an object, by its possibilities. I thought of the Rosetta stone, of certain polished agates reputed to have magical properties, of touchstones and sucking stones, worry stones, wart stones, and mad stones, wondering how I could use a bezoar in my magic act, along with Borogove and the abracadabra. The trick of pulling a stone from the viscera by sleight of hand was as ancient as mountebankery itself, and making the same stone disappear again was the stock-in-trade of prestidigitation. All of this was irresistible to me and the lime twig of my undoing.

Even the name was a talisman, derived from Persian *bãdzahr, pãdzahr: pãd* (protecting against) plus *zahr* (poison). Avenzoar, whose real name was ibn-Zohr, believed the wondrous stone was the poison of serpents eaten by stags and excreted as tears that coagulated and dropped from their eyes. Paolo Boccone's *The Teeth of Petrified Poisons* (Amsterdam, 1674) took a similar approach. Moses Maimonides praised it as an antipestilential electuary in times of plague, and al-Kindi offered a written recommendation of it as a powerful cure (with the help of Allah) in the *Aqrābādhin* (Medical Formulary) of ninth-century Baghdad. This and more from Vernell's report.

She was steeped in the scholarship of bezoars, reeling off Latin terms like *lapis bezoar orientale* for the Persian goat stone. The guanaco stone was called an occidental or western bezoar. The German bezoar came from the gemsbok. She cited Johann Wittich's testimony to the intestinal concretion's medicinal virtues in *Bericht von den wunderbaren bezoardischen Steinen* (Leipzig, 1589). She explained the deep theological implications of bezoars extracted from sacrificial rams in ancient cultures, said the Hebrews concealed bezoars in phylacteries worn during religious services, and supported her assertions with Mishnaic tradition as it appeared in Talmudic law.

I was amazed by her erudition. This was a new Vernell I was seeing for the first time. I had seen the old one with Horak at Mac's Drive-In and wasn't impressed, but this person I wanted to know. Horak, dedicated to a cult of the body, spent his time flexing and boasting about his sexual exploits. Clearly Vernell possessed depths Horak never guessed. I decided while she was still putting away her father's collection that I would talk with her. So I rushed out after class and approached her before she got away or was taken off by Horak.

'Vernell,' I blurted out, 'how'd you discover all of those details?'

She looked at me for a moment. It was the first time I ever spoke to her. Then she broke into a grin. 'Did you like it?'

'Are you kidding? Amazing stuff. Where'd it come from?'

'Dad's library. What's the use of books in the house if you don't use them? Come over sometime and I'll show you what's there.'

I didn't wait for some vague time. 'How about getting together to cram for our test over bones?' I stopped, a little out of breath, and added, 'I could use the help.'

'You, Penrod? Since when?'

'No, I'm serious. We could run through it a few times. Drill ourselves on name, rank, and location, then feed it back like brainwashed
soldiers and ace that test. What say?'

She was curious by then. Her parted lips revealed a slight overbite,
not bad, but there, as she looked at me and tried to read a motive in
my face.

'Sure, why not come over this afternoon. Nobody's home.'

'Really? I mean, what about Horak?'

'Don't worry about that. But come early enough to do some good.'
My grin must have sealed the compact because she smiled and said,
'See you then.'

I wasn't through though. Not yet. Before she turned away I asked,
'Can I touch one?'

I was gazing at the box of calculi she held in both arms against her
bodice when I said it, but I raised my eyes to her face just in time to
see her smile fall away, replaced by a look of surprise. She glanced
down at her breasts and said, 'Touch one?'

'I mean could I take one out and hold it—'

For a moment it looked like she was going to drop the box, but the
words kept coming. I wasn't sure I could wait and didn't want to miss
the chance that was before me.

'—just for a second?'

'Hold what?'

'One of your bezoars.'

Her burst of laughter brought a flush of heat to my face, but she
seemed pleased. 'Help yourself, Penrod. My hands are full.'

She held the box out to me, and from it I took a ball composed of
interlaced hairs and organic cement. I turned this over in my hand and
admired its rough texture. It was the size of a walnut and the colour of
cured tobacco, a vivid, concrete object, coherent, significant, the very
essence of a wizard's stone.

'Nice,' I said and put it back. 'See you after school.'

She was still looking at me, smiling once again, but she was already
moving away. 'Don't stand me up,' she kidded.

'I'll be there.'

After school, I hurried over to the Trigg place on Chapman Ranch

Road, where her father had his practice and facilities to stable a few horses. His office, medical library, animal clinic, and stables formed a compound apart from the house.

Vernell had a brother named Ben two grades behind us. I'd seen him around some, but only knew him by sight. It was true, though, the more I saw of him, the more I thought he was trying to imitate Horak. But he had his friends, she had hers, and there wasn't much mixing between students at different levels. Except for the seniors who dated girls from the lower grades. The brother wasn't around when I got there. Only Vernell.

She took me by the hand, saying, 'Come here, I'll show you.'

And she accompanied me out past the stables to the clinic, passing through it and going into the library, where the bezoars were displayed in a glass case for knickknacks. I stopped by the case and glanced at the room, at the big table, at the books lining the four walls. From one of the shelves she removed a thick volume and put it on the table. It was a copy of *Gray's Anatomy,* but at that moment only the bezoars on display could hold my attention.

Arranged by size, shape, and colour, each specimen had a card with the kind of animal it came from and the native range of that animal written on it. Some bezoars were halved to show their cores. Some were perfectly formed spheres. With the exception of Antarctica every continent was represented by yellow, brown, or blue gallstones, urinary calculi that looked like the fossilized gray cortex of pygmies or black coprolite from ancient imaginary beings. One pure white hemisphere, cut like a geode and exposing a nail core surrounded by concentric layers of calcified mineral salts, could have been a paperweight.

Several were formed from the fine undercoat of Bolivian vicuñas and crystallized esters. A fruit stone, perhaps the undigested pit of a date, gave its shape to a dromedary bezoar about four inches long and slightly enlarged at one end. Baling wire was the nucleus of another. There was no way of knowing, without breaking them open, how many goat bezoars owed their existence to olive pits, peaches, plums, or persimmons. One rare item resembled a tiny drumlin, as if a replica of some vestigial ridge of glacial drift. An oversized red calculus might have been the gallstone of a woolly mammoth. The pulverized minerals of this mother lode, Vernell had told us, would have given the apothecary of Baghdad a year's supply of the elephant bile which, with Allah's help, cured melancholia, ringworm, and the deadly sting of certain scorpions.

'Sit there,' she said, pulling out a chair at the big table.

She took the one to my left. *The entire skeleton in the adult consists of two hundred distinct bones.* These opening words introduced us to the human skeleton and our task. So with *Gray's Anatomy* as a guide we went through the major bones once, then gave her first go at naming them without the aid of a text.

I would be the skeleton, the *Anatomy* open before me to monitor her performance.

Perfect on the cranium and the bones of the face, producing names and locations without a hitch, she continued her placing method by touching my collar bone and saying, 'Clavicle.' Then she dropped her hand to my upper arm and added to the list, 'Humerus.'

'That's right.'

She took my elbow and ran her finger along that bone to the wrist. 'Ulna, so named for forming the elbow.' Felt the top bone of my forearm. 'Radius.'

'Right.'

Her fingers were on the back of my hand, but she went back to the wrist. 'Carpus, metacarpus,' she said, returning to the previous spot.

We had taken the calculated risk of learning only the segments of the hand and not each bone. It was a chance, but not much of one. We didn't believe Coach Smiley would give a test with questions about all two hundred bones. There wouldn't be time enough to take the test.

She turned my palm up and took hold of my fingers, one at a time, then held my thumb. 'Phalanges.'

'Perfect,' I said.

'Did you ever suck your thumb?'

'I don't know.' I thought a moment. 'Maybe. I can't remember.'

'I did.'

'Really?'

'Until old enough for school. I didn't want to stop then, but my mom said I'd have to wear braces if I didn't.

Her gaze drifted towards the books along the far wall, and she was staring into space, lost in thought. I waited, watching her expression, her breathing, lowering my eyes to the same jersey top she had on at school, and suddenly her nipples, as vivid as raised cleats, were straining against the fabric. What I saw gave me a jolt, causing me to shift in my seat. I lifted my head and saw her staring at me.

'What?' she asked.

'I didn't say anything.'

'No, but—' Her look questioned me. '—you were thinking.'

My hand was clenched in a hitchhiker's fist held by her on the table. She gave me a wry smile, slipped her fingers down to the ball at the base of my thumb, then ran the edge of her polished nails up the extended length, barely grazing it. And still her look questioned.

'You have no idea what it's like, do you?'

'What?'

'Sucking your thumb.'

'No.'

Uncomfortable, aware my hands weren't as rough as the hands of other guys, I looked at the soft white flesh, thought of overheard comments about the cutest little fat people, and felt exposed. She bent toward the table, looking at my hand. I didn't know what she was doing. My mind wasn't wandering, but for an instant I found myself staring at the table supporting our hands, my gaze fixed on its surface, on the whorls in the oak grain. At that moment they might have been visible signs of the chaos I was feeling.

The tip of her tongue parted her lips, moistening them. I started to draw my hand back, but she held it firmly against the grain and went down, her mouth opening, taking me inside, her lips closing slowly over the inert flesh. There was no looking at the table or *Gray's Anatomy*. No thinking of bones or tests. I felt the warmth. I felt the pull as she sucked, swallowed, trying to take me into her throat, came up, rolled her tongue over the end, and plunged it back inside.

I could see her face and throat in profile, her eyes closed, could feel the tug like a riptide pulling me out to sea, could see the movement of her throat when she swallowed. Dazed, staring openmouthed, I made the effort to shut my mouth and managed somehow, though without pulling away. I couldn't move.

When she came off, her eyes were closed and she was smiling, apparently pleased. There was a prolonged moment of silence. Then she opened her eyes and looked at me.

'Now you know.'

'There must be more to it.'

She nodded. 'There's more. You just don't remember, but you sucked your thumb. Like everyone else. Before you were born. Before you ever breathed.'

'You're right. I don't remember.'

'The difference is some of us did it long enough to remember.' She laughed. 'Know what a succubus is?'

'No. What's a succubus?'

'A demon in the form of a woman that comes to you in the night while you're sleeping.'

'And?'

'Visits you carnally, so to speak.'

'This is a myth, right?'

'Penrod, the high school magician—' She arched her brow and gave me that wry smile again. '—you're not turning your nose up at myths, spirits, and magic, are you?'

She had me there – if I wanted to have any credibility at all.

'I'd bet,' she said, 'if we only knew, there's a connection—' She let the thought trail off.

'Connection?'

'Between the sucking instinct and myths of vampires and succubi.'

I shook my head. Unsuspected depths. From there we went back to the bones. She handled the long bones – femur, tibia, fibula, tarsus, metatarsal – as well as she had earlier handled the occipital, parietal, and maxillary, but we'd had enough by the time we got to the toes and called it quits. As I was going out she called me back to the glass case, which she opened. She took out the tobacco-coloured bezoar and held it out.

'Lapis bezoar orientale,' she said. 'Take it, Penrod, in case a succubus ever tries to put a carnal kiss on you while you're asleep.'

I took it with me and began to practice palming it, making it disappear and reappear, like the coins older men pull from the ears of young children. When Coach Smiley gave us the test he remained true to form and kept the number of questions at an even one hundred. We had figured right.

Over the weekend my father set me to work mowing and clearing away brush on a lot at Lake Corpus Christi. By that evening I had a bad itch on my forearms and the next day an ugly itching rash. Poison ivy or oak. I never saw which. I applied calamine lotion and was wearing a long-sleeve shirt Monday when Horak, with Mansheim and Hooter, stopped me in the hall.

'So, Penrod,' Horak said, 'you going out to Vernell's these days. What would you two have in common?'

'We study,' I said.

'Why would she want a fatty to study with?'

'Good grades, Horak. They help in school?'

'Hear that?' he said, turning to his pals. 'Penrod the brain is turning Vernell's head.'

Hooter leered at me and wagged his hand like it had just been burned. 'Hot stuff.'

'Wrong stuff,' Horak said. 'Vernell likes her trade a little rougher. You got a cigarette, Penrod?'

'Never touch them.'

'No?' He patted me down, felt the bezoar in my pocket, and pulled it out. Holding it up to the light he asked, 'What do we have here? You been stealing the vet's rocks, Penny?'

'Give it here and I'll show you.' I held out my hand.

'This better be good, chubby.' He tossed it into the air.

I caught it, cupped it in both hands, made like I was slipping it up my sleeve, palmed it, and made it disappear before their eyes.

'What we have here is Penrod the wise guy.'

He grabbed my cuff, unbuttoned it, and pushed up the sleeve. When he saw the nasty rash on my forearm he let go and backed off. Likewise Hooter and Mansheim.

'What are you, a carrier?'

'Me?' I looked at my arm. 'That's nothing but scabies.'

'Is it catching?'

I gave my rash a long thoughtful look before saying, 'I'm not sure if it's past the contagious stage or not. I was curing it with what you took from me, but nothing happened. We'll know soon enough, since you had the bezoar, whether it cures or passes the disease on.'

'Get back. Get away.'

Horak was holding his hands out, palms up, fingers spread, moving toward the men's room across the hall when I last saw him. He'd be late to class as usual, but this time for a good cause. His hands would be as clean as repeated scrubbings could get them, and there was always something to be said for cleanliness.

I found Coach Smiley returning the tests and praising Vernell, who wasn't there, for making a perfect score – one hundred correct answers out of a possible one hundred. Afterward I asked Coach if he wanted me to take Vernell's test out to her. Might make her feel better, I suggested, which was exactly the right thing to say because he was actually a nice guy underneath the macho posturing.

No one answered at the house. So I went around to the compound and saw her brother, Ben, climbing the outside ladder leading to the hayloft. The structure was a modern complex of horse stalls and storage, made of metal, substantial by any standard. When I yelled at him he looked around and brought a hand to his mouth, signalling for quiet. My voice hadn't been that loud. He came down and walked over.

'Vernell around?' I asked.

He had a smug look on his face. 'Sure, Penrod, she's here. You want to see her?'

'I've got something for her.'

Studying me a moment as if trying to make up his mind he finally said, 'Okay, but stay behind me and keep it quiet.'

Waving me forward he turned and went up the ladder. I followed. In the loft we climbed steps of stacked bales to a dizzying height among the steel beams and support stanchions that gave a partial view of the stalls below and the glossy rumps of stabled horses. Dust motes on a gentle current drifted into the slanted bar of light from the after-noon sun, floating, turning like plankton, and drifted out of the light, an endless stream appearing from and disappearing into the shadows of the dim barn. In the dimness there was nothing to see or, I should say, there was nothing of note that I could see.

Ben gestured toward a niche at the far end of the building, where more hay was stacked. I shut my eyes. I opened them and saw Horak – half sitting, half standing – against a hip-high bale of hay. His face was red and screwed up, eyes closed, mouth stretched wide, teeth clenched in a tormented expression.

'What's wrong with him?'

'Look. There,' Ben said, pointing. 'Just in front of him.'

I squinted against the dimness and saw nothing. Again I shut my eyes, trying to hurry their adjustment to the changing light. When I looked the second time I thought I detected movement slightly above the top edge of the bale Horak was behind. 'What is it?'

'Vernell.'

'Vernell? What's she doing?'

'What do you think she's doing, Penrod?'

I stared at Horak's pained grimace, summoning the image of Vernell's face bent over my hand. I saw her in the library, eyes shut, lips closed over my thumb. Each swallow was visible in the contractions of her throat, irresistibly felt like an oceanic undertow sucking me out to sea. I saw the sea stretching to the horizon. I saw swimmers caught in the changing tide, its unrelenting force pulling them under. I heard desperate, unanswered cries. The cries of tormented souls, I thought, visited by a succubus in the night. I saw a black widow breaking the gossamer bonds that held her, sucking the essence from the living body of her mate. I saw the fluids being drained from him. I saw the kiss of a spider woman. I saw a man eating a gallbladder pulled from the body of a living hooded cobra. I saw the sap rising through the veins of leaves and watched the cobra venom coagulate into a stone that passed through the man to be deposited on an altar of gold.

I remembered boasts by boys in the showers at school. I remembered the cryptic words of Janice the Torch, whispered in the back of the bus after school one day. She waited, watching me a long time, as if trying to figure something out, before turning away, her mind made up. As the images crowded in on me I reached for my bezoar, afraid that I would always be imprisoned by all that I had seen, and wondered later how I got out of there without falling and hurting myself or remembering whether Ben left with me or not.

My fear was justified. Horak's grimace haunted me for years after that, in dreams, his distorted face coming to me at night as I was pursued by faceless creatures. To the point that I dreaded going to sleep. I became an insomniac, carried the bezoar with me everywhere and at all times. When I had to sleep I kept it under the pillow. My appetite diminished and I was at last able to shed the baby fat I believed I would never lose. I grew thin.

High school was long behind me when my dentist said I needed to have my wisdom teeth pulled. Afraid of sodium pentothal I wouldn't let him put me under. I was afraid of what I might say, afraid I might never wake up. So his dental assistant used nitrous oxide and shot my gums full of novocaine. Always tense in the dentist chair, I held the bezoar and stroked it for comfort until the laughing gas and novocaine could take effect. Under the cone and the chemical influence I grew euphoric.

The attractive dental assistant had her hand in my mouth, my lips stretched wide as she positioned the stays for taking x-rays and had me clamp down. Teeth clenched I watched her leave the room. While she was out of the room I thought, if only I had used nitrous oxide every day of my life I would have loved everyone. Lying there, feeling wonderful, stroking my sacred talisman, I wanted the attractive girl to return and put her hand back in my mouth. Without the stays, able to talk, I would have offered to suck her thumb. I seemed to soar, to leave my body. As I rose above the chair, looking down on myself, I saw the same grimace that had been on Horak's face and in my dreams countless times. I was dazed. Because I didn't feel tormented at all.

I felt loved by all. I felt love for everyone, for Vernell, for Horak, for Vernell's brother, Ben, for Mansheim and Hooter, Coach Smiley, even for myself. At that moment I would have welcomed the company and the carnal kiss of a succubus who came to me in the night. I would have revelled in it, shared it, returned it, and hoped against all hope that it would never end.

Keeping Mum

At one o'clock on Saturday I bring mum a plate of lemon curd sandwiches and a bottle of Guinness. Mum hasn't been feeling well lately. I shake the blankets gently.

'Wake up, mum. I need the shopping money.'

The way mum looks at me I think she's angry. But then she sees the tray and smiles.

'You're a good boy, Pete. Bring mummy her handbag.'

By the time I find her handbag, mum is sitting up in bed, pouring her Guinness. She drinks half the glass, then looks into her handbag for her purse. She pulls out a few crumpled pounds and a fiver.

'I'll write you a note,' she says. 'Because mummy needs cigarettes.'

I count the money. There's not enough to buy any meat, but I don't say anything.

'No need to open the curtains,' says mum.

*   *   *

Coming back from the shops I see Mr Manley and his son William standing in their front garden. Mr Manley is holding a spade. It looks new. The blade is clean and shiny.

'Watch me now,' he tells William. He looks back at his house then squints at the low brick wall at the end of the garden. 'This should do it.' He grips the spade's maroon plastic handle, places his boot on the blade and pushes down. The spade disappears into the soil.

*   *   *

Mum comes downstairs while I am watching *Z Cars*. She is wearing a red dress. Her wig swirls around her head like an advert for hair spray.

'I'm just nipping out,' she says. 'Shan't be long.'

*   *   *

I am walking down the street, kicking through leaves, looking for conkers. It is Sunday afternoon. *The Big Match* is over. Mum called this morning to say she had spent the night at Aunt Phoebe's. 'I had one of my turns,' she said.

There aren't many conkers about. It is still too early in the year. Mr Manley and William come out and start digging their hole again. I sit on their garden wall and watch. At first, Mr Manley does all the work. He makes grunting sounds each time he sticks the spade into the ground. Before long his face is purple. William watches. His face is covered in spots. Mum says he has a rhubarb and custard complexion. He has a few wispy hairs sprouting from his chin. Bumfluff, mum calls it.

The hole is getting deep. Mr Manley opens the front of his jacket and steps inside to continue digging. A conker shell falls from a nearby tree and I move towards the sound. I decide to walk around the block to investigate the horse chestnut trees on Milton Avenue.

*   *   *

Twenty minutes later I am walking home, pockets bulging. Mr Manley is leaning on his spade as William tries to shovel earth from the hole with a garden fork. 'Come on lad,' says Mr Manley as the soil crumbles through the fork and falls back into the hole.

Upstairs in my bedroom I line my conkers along the window sill, counting them as I go. I take my brown shoe box down from the shelf. I remove my notebook and on a new page write down the date and the number of conkers I have gathered. I use my notebook to keep track of all my conker fights, fist fights, soccer games, running times and the amounts I win or lose playing penny up the wall. Everything is coded so no one else can understand what anything means.

*   *   *

Mum comes home at seven o'clock. She has left her wig at Aunt Phoebe's and one of her stiletto heels is broken. She says she has an awful migraine and goes upstairs to lie down. At eight o'clock I take her up some beans on toast and a bottle of Guinness.

*   *   *

It rains on Monday and mum's rheumatism keeps her in bed. When I get home from school I watch *Blue Peter* and *The Magic Roundabout* and the news and *Nationwide.* At half-past six Mr Manley delivers a box from the off licence. He carries it into the kitchen, unpacks the bottles and replaces them with the empties. I give him the money. When he gets to the front door he turns and pulls a Mars bar from his pocket.

'They were all out of Crunchies,' he says.

At half-past seven I make fried eggs and fried bread for dinner.

On Tuesday I make fish fingers and buttered bread.

On Wednesday I make cheese and pickle sandwiches.

On Thursday mum is out when I get home and I can't get in because the back door is locked. I walk around to the front of the house and see William Manley in his front garden. He is standing looking into the hole. I climb over the wall that separates our gardens, walk over to where he is standing and look down where he is looking. The hole is dark and clammy, ten times deeper than any hole I ever dug. Apart from that, there's not much else to see.

'My dad's crazy,' says William. 'Come inside. I'll show you something.'

We go into the house. I follow William upstairs, into his father's bedroom. William climbs over the bed and opens a drawer on the other side. He holds up a magazine. On the cover is a picture of a naked woman holding her hands over her bosoms. The magazine's name is *Mayfair,* the most expensive place you can buy in Monopoly. William lies on the bed and begins flicking through the pages.

'Look at that,' he says, pointing at a bus conductress who is not wearing any underwear.

'Cor,' he says, looking at several pictures of a woman lying naked on a sofa. The woman's hair is blonde, but the hair between her legs is dark brown.

'Look at those tits,' says William.

*   *   *

When I go back home the back door is unlocked and mum is in bed. I make us a pile of toast and marmalade.

'Thanks, Pete, you're a rock,' says mum. She sits up in bed and pours her Guinness. 'Maybe I'll be well enough to get up tomorrow.'

*   *   *

When I come home on Friday, mum is sitting on the sofa pouring tea for a strange man in a blue suit.

'Hallo, Peter,' she says. 'You remember Uncle Ronnie.'

We all drink tea and eat slices of swiss roll. Then mum says she is going to walk Uncle Ronnie to the station. I do the washing up then turn on the telly to watch the end of *Crackerjack*.

*   *   *

.At one o'clock on Saturday I bring mum a plate of lemon curd sandwiches and a bottle of Guinness. She gives me the money for the shopping and a note for her cigarettes.

When I go outside, Mr Manley is already digging. William is standing watching, picking at the spots on his chin and pulling at his bumfluff. Only Mr Manley's top half is visible. He grunts every time he heaves a shovelful of earth to the surface.

Mr Manley hands William the spade then heaves himself out of the hole. He waves me over. The three of us stand looking down, like astronauts at the edge of a crater. A worm slithers into view and plops down to the bottom of the hole. I would like to take it home and cut it in two to see if both halves survive, but I don't say anything.

'I'm making a pond,' Mr Manley says, placing his hand on my shoulder. 'With goldfish and lilies. It'll be magic when it's finished.'

*   *   *

When I get home from the shops the back door is open. I call mum but she doesn't answer. I unpack the shopping then go out to look for conkers. I walk down the road and around to Milton Avenue. I fill my pockets then come home and line up my conkers on the window sill, counting them as I go. I take down my shoe box and get out my notebook and the doorbell rings.

I go downstairs and it is William.

'My dad said to get you,' he says.

I follow him over the wall that separates our gardens. Mr Manley is looking into the hole, talking to himself. Then I get to the hole and mum is sitting inside it, naked.

'Hallo, Pete,' she says. 'I fell in a hole.'

I can't move, so I just stand there. Mum is smiling at the sky. I look at Mr Manley and he looks at me. William is staring at my mum.

"Born free," mum starts singing.

I turn and run back to our house and up to mum's room. I open her wardrobe and begin pulling out skirts and dresses and blouses. I take bras and underwear and tights from her chest of drawers. I grab a wig and a head scarf and a pair of movie star dark glasses. I throw these things onto the bed, bundle them into a sheet and hurry back to the Manley's garden.

MICHAEL FELD

Gover's Toytown

At first Gover blamed the soft toys.

Then he thought the cuddly chimps, and giraffes, or even the elephants were not heavy and anyway only a tiny toad had recently moved off the shelves. His wife, hostile to all things cuddlesome, repeatedly urged they make way for dreary aids to numeracy, and when she did, he wondered whether the tiredness resulted from the self-abuse he practised, like so many married men, as a form of self-defence.

But this onanism was no new adventure and exhaustion never previously its legacy, and one evening after he shut the shop Gover decided to boost morale with a visit to the drunken doctor.

The dipsomaniac always slurred the same semi-comatose greeting from the examination couch on which he lay spreadeagled.

'Mr Rover! Just the man I want to see. Only patient on the register with a dog's name. Most of them lead a dog's life. None, except you, have a dog's name. Thus there is a sublime symmetry in your assuming a duty for which, frankly, I am no longer physically capable, a task which has reduced me to looking and feeling like a dying duck in a thunderstorm. The role I refer to Mr Rover, is the satisfying of the prodigious carnal appetite of the landlady of The Dog & Duck. Understand? You dog, me duck, The Dog & Duck. It all fits.' Proferring the bottle of scotch he grasped by the neck the drunk doctor invariably continued 'Better get into practice. The landlady enjoys a proper drink nearly as much as a proper length. Anyway, a chap needs a swig or two before he tangles with a woman who sucks him in, then blows him out in little bubbles . . .'

The familiar fantastic soliloquy breezily despatched catarrh, pinkeye and ear wax in the past, and Gover priced it odds-on to eliminate current lethargy.

But when he arrived at the surgery, the nurse revealed, between stifled giggles, that the GP was drying out in a clinic somewhere, and Gover saw a female locum, different in more than gender from the medicine man she understudied.

Gover compared his symptoms to damp cloths, wet flannels, and limp rags, yet the locum, instead of nodding off, carried on like an Israelite at a Moses debriefing, raptly wagging ears and popping eyes and sagging jaws, before touting, in hushed tones and capital Ts, *Tests*.

'Space age technology . . . Tests . . . teaching hospital . . . where they discovered penicillin . . . Tests . . . soon as possible . . . Tests' said the locum, scribbling dynamically. 'Meantime, here's a pick-me-up.'

Gover accepted the prescription. Tablespoon of tonic following meals, he seethed listlessly, what a pathetic substitute for lashings of The Famous Grouse!

*   *   *

'I laid out nut cutlet and watercress an hour ago' huffed his wife, on the doorstep, tapping her watch like a referee furious at delaying tactics. 'Now I'm late for birth control counselling.'

Gover massaged her tendency to mollycoddle Planet Earth in a ploy to win house points. 'Stuck at the garage' he burbled mendaciously, 'analysing methods to convert the van to unleaded petrol.'

'Methods! It's a ten minute tinker' sneered Mrs Gover authoratatively, leaving Gover to his own devices as she hurried to proselytize on behalf of the contraceptive variety.

One nibble of nut cutlet sent Gover fleeing ponderously to the loft conversion and the stash of confectionery, originally intended for bribing dithering infants into a positive purchasing commitment, but now brought from the shop to exorcise diabolical vegetarian aftertaste. He chose sherbet dip to revive his palate and then probed again beneath the divan to extract another unlikely secret, a snapshot dating back to the year a periodical pressed readers to submit three proposals advancing the cause of Harmony In Wedlock (maximum ten words apiece, in block letters please, on the entry form at bottom of page).

1 RELY UPON HONEST APPRECIATION NOT NEGATIVE CRITICISM 2 NEVER TRY TO CHANGE YOUR PARTNER'S WAYS 3 READ A GOOD BOOK ON THE SEX SIDE OF MARRIAGE, Gover's inspirational trio, cast a spell over the panel of divorced celebrities sitting in judgement, and won the major Florida-for-two-plus-free-day-in-Disneyworld prize.

'When I think of America I think of smog and H Bombs and the annihilation of Red Indians' niggled Mrs Gover at news of the triumph. 'Anyway on the dates offered I am committed to a Dyslexia In Counting seminar.' Gover, imagining the excursion to Disneyworld, pined again for the child she perversely prohibited, on the grounds that one of her own would limit the good she did for everyone else's, and in an effort to fill the gap, invited a six year old trying to decide between a bag of marbles or two of balloons.

'Sherbet is one thing Mr Gover — transatlantic travel, however, is going too far!' cried the customer's mum. 'Such an inducement substantiates my worst suspicions — you're a weirdo!'

So Gover, sugar daddy manqué, journeyed in isolation to The Chantilly Paramount, smartest hotel in Key Biscayne, and there, in the lobby, was a girl, swimming in a tank.

She was beautiful the girl in the tank.

She flailed lovely long arms, she kicked lovely long legs, she swished long blonde mermaid hair, she blew bubbles out of a gilded snorkel all the men wished were them.

One afternoon, as she dripped off duty, torso poured into one-piece halter-necked costume, the crucifix sinking into her canteloupe cleavage brought home to Gover a disturbingly unchristian element in his behaviour. Lone occupant of vast double room, equipped with extravagantly surplus-to-requirement twin baths, he selfishly condemned the girl, at the end of a strenuous session in the tank, to communal showers adjacent to heart-shaped swimming pool. Eager to make amends, he tracked her to palm-treed poolside, tentatively reached for a cold shoulder and pentitently gabbled 'Please do not take me for a weirdo' because Customer's Mum's tongue had left a livid scar.

'That's the wildest accent I evah did hear' the girl declared, beaming big bleached American teeth, and an emboldened Gover dredged forth his ideas about ablutions.

'Gimme that accent wild man' said the girl, 'and we'll share jest everything you wanna.'

Through frosted panes Gover broadcast to the soapy sponging girl inside information relating to St Paul's Cathedral, the Changing of the Guard and Houses of Parliament.

'That accent sure sends me apeshit' said the curvaceous blur, and Gover persisted in it to suggest an international dimension to her career.

'I can state categorically' stated Gover categorically, 'despite English shortages of sophistication culminating in English shortages of tanks, your — substantial qualifications — qualify potential UK venues to instal — installations.'

'Wanna send the ole country apeshit?' asked the girl, steaming and glowing and out of the shower unit, swathed in Chantilly Paramount towelling. 'Show 'em some wild pics of my NE.'

'Any?' queried Gover, mystified.

'Nipple erection' said the girl pointedly. 'Gotta camera?'

Gover's adam's apple bobbled prominently. 'I think' he gulped, 'considering Buckingham Palace and stuff, something traditional is

England's cup of tea, particularly where a traditional Polaroid is involved'.

'Do whayya wanna wild man' said the girl, taking direction expertly, unravelling the voluminous bath robe and cagily covering bosom with forearm in the manner of a newsvendor concealing the headlines.

The relationship progressed, beyond decorous time-honoured posing, to the cocktail bar, where, perched upon gold-plated stools at the gold-plated bar, they suckled Blue Lagoons and gazed at alligators parading behind impenetrable glass, flaunting teeth even bigger and whiter than the girl in the tank's. Indeed the night prior to his Disneyworld expedition it reached a high pitch, when they consumed a bumper Blue Lagoon – admittedly through separate straws – out of the same great tureen.

*   *   *

The spectacle of children demanding money with menaces from cowed adult escorts and immediately passing it on to hucksters camouflaged as Mickey Mice and other copyrighted anthropomorphs, understandably uplifted the proprietor of Gover's Toytown, yet at the Jules Verne submarine, Disneyworld enthusiasm blunted. Perhaps the hamburger, fries, thick milk shake, the ten thousand calories for two dollars lunch bore responsibility, possibly the girl in the tank monopolised Gover's interest in aquatic activity – certainly he returned early to Key Biscayne.

'Key in use' said the concierge, smiling knowingly, and when Gover observed Do Not Disturb hanging on his door, and heard gurgles drifting through it, he smiled knowingly too. My oh my, that girl flogs the facilities so relentlessly they groan like they're oldfashioned English, he reflected, sloping along the corridor and lurking, according to the Snow White watch – the ideal Disneyworld souvenir for a girl obsessed with personal hygiene – for umpteen minutes precisely, until she emerged, bathed in smiles, if a trifle tottery on lovely long legs, arm in arm with the man who played piano in the cocktail bar. In the no time it took for the jet quick and dead quiet lift like you don't get in England to answer his call, the pianist dangled Gover's key down the girl's titties and with every dangle she beamed broadly, and Gover, Good Samaritan turned good loser, mused I must hand it to the piano player, his distinctive tickling of the ivories amidst the ambience of cavorting alligators emphasised most subtly the fragility of existence. And as the lift whisked the pair away Gover rebuked himself for ignoring his wife's advice to avoid fast fatty American food and also for turning down the Jules Verne submarine which the dwarf watchseller decked out as Dopey – or was it Grumpy? – praised to the sky.

Gover finally ceased lurking and musing and rebuking.

Gover finally retrieved his key from the concierge know-all.

Gover finally stumbled back into his room.

Oh Gosh, talk about the desecration of charitable innocence!

The rampant injustice of a rumpled bed she had not the common decency to unrumple! The extravagantly disloyal reek of twin bath shower gel – the stench of which girls in tanks normally never get a whiff!

Small wonder Gover sought solace in the bedside Gideon Bible.

'Where to find help when friends fail' guided him to Psalm 118.18, and 'It is better to trust the Lord than put confidence in man.'

'Humph' snorted Gover. Banality sacrilegiously straightening him out, he ordered a maid over the shark-shaped telephone and then descended to the lobby with the air of a man about to destroy his betting slips.

He knocked vigorously on the tank, laying down the law in high dudgeoned mime. 'Plans re English establishments discontinued, Repeat, discontinued. Furthermore' he asserted speechlessly, 'Blue Lagoons are over and hugely expensive huge double bathrooms are out. Repeat – over and out. End of communique. No, not the end, one other thing I forgot to mention. Mrs Gover, my spouse, will inherit the Snow White timepiece an ex-esteemed drinking partner's duplicity has forfeited.'

The girl flailed and kicked and snorkelled, humiliatingly lost for reply until they bumped into each other as Gover checked out of the hotel. Then, 'Weirdo' she hissed, foolishly swishing stringy so-called mermaid blonde locks far too violently – thus exposing mousey natural roots.

The episode accelerated the maturing process, which is why, a decade later, Gover, an accomplished man of the Disneyworld, routinely made precautions in case his wife cut Family Planning instruction surprisingly short and trapped him, treacherously ogling the image of another woman whilst simultaneously feasting off orgiastic sugar-crammed sweetmeats she castigated as poison. Discreetly turning the key in the lock, he settled on the divan, bit off the stem of a licquorice pipe, and chewed, and digested, and yawned, and like someone nobbled by tsetse fly, yawned again. He deliberately masticated the bowl of the pipe, and promising to pull himself together, he determinedly loosened his trouser belt, and allowed his mind to meander along Memory Lane, where it came across the girl in the tank's NE, and Gover closed his eyes, and did not yawn, but concentrated on the phenomenon he once so cavalierly disdained to address.

*   *   *

Thursday early closing, Gover drove his elderly, blue for a boy, pink for a girl, van into town and the hospital where they discovered penicillin in roughly the same time it took him to find a place to park. The hospital performed their Tests, and told him to come again the same time next week, and when he did he found a vacant parking meter only a half a mile from Outpatients. He'd only just finished chortling 'This is my lucky day' when the hospital said he had a very unusual complaint which nobody knew anything about, and not even penicillin could cure. The hospital did not exactly don the black cap but neither did it encourage Gover to fret over Antarctic de-icing catastrophes or nuclear dumping disasters or any of the doomsdays his wife prophesied for the fairly near future because Gover would definitely be history in the fairly near future. 'Funny' said Gover, adam's apple jerking, 'It's going to kill me, the first unusual thing I ever had.'

'Goodbye' said the hospital, meaning every word of it.

Traipsing back to his van, Gover remembered that people in his predicament were entitled to live life to the hilt. However, apart from the odd appointment with the drunken doctor and doing what he did behind the loft conversion door, he didn't have much idea how to go about it, and gratefully received the whitewashed message – in the sort of childish lettering he had selected to paint Gover's Toytown on the van – staring out of a shop window bereft of anything else.

'No body not 18 or older or shocked easy come inside. By order RBR.'

Gover teetered momentarily – then swept through the exotic beaded curtain entrance. A man sat brooding silently at the summit of a heap of publications. Undeterred, for matrimony had taught him to survive without tickertape welcomes, Gover cracked under no questioning whatever.

'I am over eighteen' he confessed.

'Scandieffinavia, Nevereffinlands, United States of Amerieffinca' the morose man suddenly intoned. 'Rare Book Ronny imeffinports from em all but does Rare Book Ronny get the Queen's Award for Indeffinustry? Effino. His unique product is coneffinscated.' He slithered down the heap, a disconsolate Guy escaping the bonfire. 'This is what they left, nufeffin unique. Like "Snatch"' he said, flinging a copy clawed from the pile.

'Snatch?' said Gover.

'Nuffin uneffinique. Same as "Muff"' said the the man, slinging.

'Muff?' said Gover.

'No uniqueness wiv "Beaver" neiver' said the man, chucking a sample.

'Beaver' said Gover, thinking cuddly toys.

'Coneffinsumers do not go the lengff and breaff of Eureffinope for "Snatch" or "Muff", nor "Beaver" or – "Pussy"' the man said, tossing. 'Nuffin's got less uneffiniqueness than "Pussy".'

'Pussy' said Gover. A bell tolled. Hadn't the drunk doctor disclosed a naughty anatomical meaning?

Gover stooped, sheepishly, slyly.

'Wasting your time' said the man. 'Rare Book Ronny knows a weirdo when he spots one. Built his trade on weirdos. What you want, troofully? Animals? Little Boys? Underage Girls?'

Gover picked up 'Pussy'. He flicked the pages.

'Gruppensex!' the man exclaimed. 'Stands out a mile, you're Gruppensex!'

Gover recognised long yellow hair, crucifix nestling in fruity cleavage.

'Hospital send yer?' said the man, animated now, unsaddened. 'You'd be ameffinazed the sickos and weirdos at the hospital'.

Gover hadn't been privy to the raised skirt, no knickers, gynaecological nether regions tittilating as terrible wounds. But mousey pubic hair provided further proof of identification.

'Rare Book Ronny's arranging a petition proteffinesting at the whole country going to the watchdogs. The bank manager's signing and this hospital coneffinsultant —'

Gover dropped 'Pussy' back on the pile. 'I suppose if you're going to discover penicillin, round here is the place to do it' he priggishly pontificated, shoving off without the common decency of a cheerio.

'Blame Obeffinscene Publication' moaned the man at swaying exotic beading. 'Weirdeffinos, never get a fankyou from any of em!'

*   *   *

She was on the doorstep again, on a mission again, tapping her watch again. 'Early closing day – and still you disrupt my canvassing schedule' she huffed. 'Doubtless it escaped your attention the local election campaign is underway.'

'Maybe it did, maybe it didn't' said Gover. His adam's apple bobbled as he thought wait till she hears what the hospital said. 'I've been stuck at —'

'Please refrain from insulting my intelligence with that garage nonsense' his wife interjected. 'A bio-yoghourt and raisin salad supper is located in the refrigerator.'

Gover glanced at the political rosette she sported in support of the party wanting everyone to have nothing more than a sense of foreboding. 'Do not try to change your partner's ways' he speechlessly recited. 'Never criticise – give –' giving up on a formula which failed to withstand the wash of time.

*   *   *

Abandoning ambition to live life to the hilt, Gover buried himself in work. The mortgage broker refused to pursue a train set enquiry for fear of electrocuting a nephew; the dry-cleaning assistant remained unconvinced paint toxicity levels were insufficient to result in fatality, should her grandson lick rather than fly a model aeroplane; the bank cashier worried his daughter might scoff the dainty replicas furnishing a doll's house.

The locum appeared too, contemplating a cuddly bear for a god-child. 'I shall need to study statistics vis-a-vis flammability ratios of the stuffing' she said.

'Will you?' said Gover, the pointless pick-me-up devoutly golloped three times daily at the root of his offhandedness.

'Current circumstances underline the importance of reducing fire hazard.'

'Really?' said Gover, not bothering to suppress a yawn.

'What with the accident' said the locum, relapsing into testy stage whispers.

'Accident?' gawped Gover indistinctly.

'To the doctor, your – former – doctor.'

'Former?' said Gover, sharpening up.

'Didn't you hear? His lady friend smuggled spirits into the rehabilitation centre'.

'"The Famous Grouse"' said Gover, at last eruditely on the ball.

'He drank the bottle, and promptly fell asleep with a lighted cigarette.'

'One of the few still loyal to Capstan Full Strength' said Gover.

'Smoke suffocated him—'

'Thought they were strong but not that strong' Gover butted in admiringly.

'—I mean smoke inhalation not burns killed him. Whilst on the subject' the locum added, briskly back to business, 'what is the percentage risk of soft toys suffocating babies?'

Gover finally surrendered hope of disposing of any item of stock. 'The risk? Oh enormous, quite enormous' he replied, thinking petitions proteffinesting at the country going to the watchdogs surplus to requirement with the watchdogs already in complete control.

'Your honesty typifies the neighbourhood's village atmosphere' applauded the locum. 'I'm quite delighted to be staying permanently.'

'Oh, permanently. That's really er all right' said Gover, the public relations man. 'By the way, I believe I can claim the right to a disabled sticker for permission to park in non-parking zones. You see the hospital said —'

'Out of the question' said the locum. 'Their findings mean you must cease motoring forthwith — think of the carnage you'd create losing consciousness at the wheel?'

'Oh' said Gover, adam's apple yo-yoing.

'Now Mr Gover, don't let yourself go' the locum reprimanded. 'There is a silver lining. The medical profession would suffer less stress if there were fewer malingerers requesting treatment and more incurables like yourself bravely adapting to the fact there isn't any.'

'Oh', said Gover, 'thanks', and recovering his public relations poise he held open the door for the locum's departure.

Outside, taking advantage of the village atmosphere, cars branded L for Learner, slid laboriously to emergency stops, grinded into incorrect gear and mutinously mounted pavements during three point turns. Adam's apple jolting, Gover dwelled bitterly on the novice drivers' inadequacies and on his abrupt banishment from the road despite a clean licence held since youth. He dawdled to the sweet shop a few doors along the parade, chose at random a packet of aniseed balls to help pull himself together and noticed the manufacturer advertising an Upside Down Faces drawing contest on the wrapping. An old competitive urge stirred. Not many with my experience and motivation will be having a go at this, Gover gloated inwardly, I swear I must have a good chance of winning this!

*   *   *

One hand clinging to virgin pad and magic markers, the other to a stair rail, Gover hauled himself to the loft conversion, but instead of genius blooming in the compost of imminent extinction as anticipated, he lolled feverishly, blocked, unartistic, utterly Upside Down Faceless, cursing his inability to turn genius on like a tap, or Mozart. Gover reckoned he should do better than Mozart. He was older for a start. Forty-odd. That's a better innings than Mozart's thirty-five. Only a moderate knock perhaps in an era brimming with space age technology, and transplants, and artificial hips etcet, but still higher than Mozart's.

Anyway, musically speaking, he preferred treacly popular airs, not that he liked the pianists who churned them out, nor the girls who jumped into bed with them. Fortunately, a shrewd business brain prevented him showering those sluts with gifts: a lawfully wedded wife remained the sole recipient of his generosity and his retailer's head stayed securely screwed on even if she rejected a present. That Snow White watch for instance, declined on the ground it symbolised exploitation of the handicapped, he successfully deployed as an incentive bonus to clinch the sale of a dolly which wore nappies and wet itself.

Memories of that plaything's power of evacuation spawned a resolve to rotate underpants frequently in readiness for exhibition at the mortuary acceptable to Mrs Gover when confirming him next of kin. In funereal felt tip he jotted on his clean white pad, clean white underwear, and lots of it, fullstop.

Strange that such an innocuous memo should spark outright rebellion.

For bold lettering, with a mind of its own, blackly asked, What does it matter, embarrassing the wife? YOU HATE YOUR WIFE, it said, bursting forth into competitive block capitals.

Exchanging harsh black for sexy scarlet, he listed the reasons.

He hated her for not allowing him to add his own bit of shrapnel to the population explosion because that would inevitably restrict her freedom to teach the new mathematics.

He hated her for teaching the new mathematics but he hated her more for teaching it to other people's children and not his own.

He hated her propaganda on behalf of the battery-operated calculator and her contempt for the ancient workmanlike abacus he still stocked.

He hated her silly wholesale concern for the world and her silly smalltime concern for the locality, and he hated her conviction she was brought into being to fulfil some purpose and he hated the energy she derived from that belief.

He hated her breasts like two poached eggs and the Desperate Dan legs she kept quite impecccably shut.

And that time in the shop, he hated her thinking the lad jabbering about the James Brothers and toting a cap gun was referring to William and Henry rather than Jesse and Frank.

Wow, Gover elaborating why he hated his wife displayed genius on a Mozartian scale, it wasn't until the wee small hours that he turned off the tap and toppled to the divan.

In the morning, he heroically didn't gag when he swallowed healthy coffee, without caffeine.

His wife, alternately glaring at him and her digital watch, signalled distaste as well. For decadent oversleepers.

Incredibly Gover retaliated. 'What you still doing here?' he asked. 'On strike?'

'You ought know full well' she spluttered venomously. 'Today is local election day and the school is occupied as a polling station.'

Gover contrived a yawn to imply disinterest.

'I suppose you might find a moment in your crowded day to exercise a basic democratic right.'

'Maybe I will' said Gover. 'Maybe I won't.'

'Nothing is more important.'

'Really?' said Gover. 'Nothing?'

'Nothing!' spat the politicised Mrs Gover, democratically distraught at the flicker of organised opposition. 'Fortunately it's early closing and you can shuttle our supporters to and from the polls.'

'Can't' said Gover. 'Van's going to the garage.'

'I won't listen to that garage nonsense' began Mrs Gover, not having to, for Gover was off and away, a wild man, exceeding speeds of 30mph, criminally not fastening his seat belt, almost refusing to let a pensioner cross at the zebra, squealing into the garage with a brutal brakeslamming emergency stop and instructing the service department, to convert the engine, regardless of time or expense, to unleaded fuel and thus minimise brain damage to the children of England.

And having done all that, he invented his own brain damage limitation scheme. He would avoid safety fanatics altogether by making early closing a never opening day.

*   *   *

She roamed the school playground, accosting the electorate, regurgitating her candidate's policies in the crucial areas of bottle banks and sleeping policemen.

'You?' she said, buttonholing her husband. 'What are you doing here this early?'

'There is nothing' smarmed Gover the wise guy, 'more important than exercising the right to vote.'

'Widdows' she hissed. 'Our man's Widdows.'

The hiss evoked the girl in the tank's farewell all those years ago, and in a secret shrouded booth, instead of Gover scratching X like an illiterate making his mark, he adopted the painstakingly primitive Toytown style of scrawl to weave 'Weirdos' the length and breadth of the election hopefuls.

He exited, bathed in smiles, thinking himself privileged to live in a society where the populace can make its protest through the ballot box. His wife, noticing his demeanour, winced, mean-mindedly smelling a rat, but Gover, normally victim of cheating and abuse, revelled in dispensing extra helpings of both. 'Weirdos' he mimed, with a vast dumb mouth movement, waving a champion's thumbs-up.

*   *   *

He left the door of the loft conversion open wide as the legs of the girl starring in 'Pussy' and unearthed the polaroid picture, and held it upside down. Magic marker inspirationally conjured long fake blonde hair into a beard and the chin, automatically, miraculously, became a bald man's pate. Gover yawned jubilantly yet cautiously opted for a breather. Well aware that unbridled brilliance is often precursor to nervous breakdown, he relaxed, prior to fleshing out the glorious concept on the pristine white sheets of his pad, flicking an obese jelly baby, the orange colour of a disabled permit, into the air, and catching it, like a flaked circus seal, in his serial yawn.

   And then, he scattered bubble gum and coconut ice and cough candy and the rest of the confectionery stash anywhere and everywhere, and collapsing to the divan, indolently mused how his will, signed and sealed, and sitting in the solicitor's safe in the High Street, granted his wife all his worldly goods, including the chunk of endowment assurance defending the house against the Grim Reaper's swipe. And prudence had organised environmental matters as well as material ones in favour of the tight, taut, boney Mrs. Next week the nearly vintage van would run in modern ozone friendly fashion and this week, next week, in no time, he would die, and that was a most discriminating way of giving, because the less people, the less waste, and pollution, and disease, and deception, and disgust.

   It takes a good deal of sophistication to comprehend all that, and cope with all that, and the thought of how grown-up he had become, and what he had done, and how much he was leaving the wife, put him to sleep, quickly and quietly as an elevator at The Chantilly Paramount, smartest hotel in Key Biscayne.

Ted Walker

NOT FAR FROM SYDNEY

In Rookwood Cemetery there is a stone
That bears a plangent, one-word epitaph.
It isn't ever done, when you're alone
Among old graves, to have a quiet laugh

At death, or dying – Least of all, the dead:
Their disassembled bones might shake aghast
Below your crass, clodhopping mirth. Instead,
You think how life slips by, your wasted past

Regretted, irretrievable, and sigh,
And frown, and wonder what to do with time

That's left (not much) before you, too, must die.
What can be said? Little, save the sublime,

Chiselling, monumental mason's truth
Monosyllabically implied in *STREWTH!*

Gavin Ewart

HORSES (August 1914)

As the hordes of Huns came, streaming down from Belgium,
with GOTT MIT UNS emblazoned on belt buckles,
French and Germans, British, all were gallivanting,
before they settled down and were fastened in long trenches,
across the hot and lovely countryside of farmyards,
on the cared-for backs of the beautiful sleek horses . . .

horses, once three-toed ones (Hipparion, Protohippus),
striped foals still reminding of the camouflage of forests,
that had been men's allies (if you counted) years in thousands.
Horses were in battle long before our Hastings,
pawing, whinnying, neighing, charging at the hated
fearful opposition of the axe and heavy broadsword . . .

Ancestors of men, and the ancestors of horses,
shared the beastly burden of the necessary murder,
legs were lopped and broken, bodies pierced and battered,
jaws hung loose, lopsided; cannon bashed them piecemeal,
terror drove them crazy, there was high-pitched screaming,
hysteria of horses – the loved, admired élite ones . . .

Generals had horses (Wellington had Copenhagen),
the men in charge of horses all truly loved their horses.
But this was worst of all, in that hot retreating August –
never before such chaos, such noise, mind-blowing shellbursts;
turning guns, to drag them over slippery rail tracks.
This was their last and worst war, Armageddon of the horses.

ZEBRA HYBRIDS
— see *The Penycuik Experiments* by James Cossar Ewart (1899)

It's nice to think of his foals:
Romulus, Remus, Brenda,
Norette and Heckla —
bright, intelligent little things,
ready to rush away with the herd
as soon as born,
expecting lions,
frightened of lengths of rope (snakes!).

Quicker off the mark than a horse or a donkey,
yellow and orange, black-striped,
whose remote ancestor was perhaps Hipparion
(horses were descended straight from Protohippus,
my grandfather thought).

The sire in each case was a Burchell's zebra.
The dams were (in order): a West Highland pony
from the Island of Rum
(suspected forebears from the Spanish Armada);
a three parts bred 14.1 hands Irish mare;
a cross-bred Clydesdale mare;
a good-looking eleven hands Shetland pony;
a twelve hands skewbald Iceland pony.

So what about Lord Morton's 1815ish
crossing a mare of pure blood with a quagga?
What about telegony?
The theory that a previous sire infected the bloodstream
so that in the dam you would find 'saturation'
and traces of a previous sire in a later mating.
They spoke all the time of 'infection'.
Even Darwin veered towards telegony,
and all the breeders of race-horses believed in it.
They shuddered at the thought of zebrules and zebrinnies.

So what about Lady Meux, Sir Gore Ouseley,
Wilfrid Scawen Blunt, Sir Everett Millais –
for whom the words 'good breeding' must have meant something?

Zebras are hard to train, they're naturally timid,
though they're very hardy.
Horses succumb to the bite of the tsetse fly . . .
They wanted a hybrid that won't work in Africa.

But by the late 80s Daimler and Benz
had invented the internal combustion engine, and put it on the road.
The first petrol-driven car came to England in 1888, a three-wheeler.
Completely immune to the tsetse fly
and fairly easy to manage (also, not afraid of snakes).

The little zebra hybrids all died young, of Strongylus thread-worm
and never arrived at maturity . . .

So it's a story, altogether, of a sad frustration.
But at least my grandfather tried.

ANCESTOR WORSHIP

My grandfather always ate his porridge
standing, with his back to the wall.
This was in honour of the clansmen –
to avoid being stabbed in the back.

He was an Edinburgh professor,
perhaps he also thought of colleagues –
inching in, to knife him?

I didn't like so much salt in the porridge,
I did my best to swamp it with sugar . . .

The Strange
Fate of
Aimé Bonpland

According to Avé-Lallemant, who visited him in 1858, Aimé Bonpland ate with his fingers, and didn't wear shoes. He was 85 years old, and had just fathered three children with an Indian mistress. He lived like a gaucho, with straw hat and poncho, on the Uruguay river on a farm at Paso de Santa Ana, far from any city. Yet this same octogenarian had become a celebrity after travelling five years round South America with Alexandre von Humboldt from 1799 to 1804. He had met on equal terms with the luminaries of his day from Chateaubriand to Sir Joseph Banks, and Charles Darwin had called him 'the best of judges'. He also befriended the South American liberator Simón Bolívar, and was twice awarded the Légion d'Honneur. Empress Joséphine appointed him head gardener at the Malmaison; he became her confidant, married one of her friends, and cried when she died. In 1843 Thomas Carlyle alluded to Bonpland's strange fate:

The whole world knows of M. Aimé Bonpland; how Francia seized him, descending on his tea-establishment in Entre Ríos, like an obscene vulture, and carried him off into the interior, contrary even to the law of the nations; how the great Humboldt and other persons expressly applied to Dr Francia, calling on him, in the name of human Science . . . to liberate M. Bonpland; and how Dr. Francia made no answer, and M. Bonpland did not return to Europe, or indeed has never yet returned . . .

Yet despite this fame Bonpland vanished into obscurity in the hinterlands of Argentina, leaving no written testimony of his errant life. When I read that he had been murdered by a gaucho I decided to find out how that had happened.

The absence of revealing diaries, or autobiographic fragments, indeed an aversion to writing, meant that other people's insights would be the main way into Bonpland's life and mind. His close

(*Aimé Bonpland, por Pellegrini.*)

friend and travelling companion Alexandre von Humboldt became my first source. Humboldt, aged 29, met Bonpland, aged 25, in Revolutionary Paris in 1798 at the hotel Boston where both lodged. They were due to join Capt Baudin's Directorate financed world tour but war with Austria intervened. After a fruitless wait in Marseille hoping to join Napoleon in Egypt, they travelled together to Spain, and then to Spanish America. All Bonpland's expenses were met by Humboldt. In the Spanish Government passport he was Humboldt's 'ayudante' or secretary. During the five-year voyage Bonpland seems to have been as sturdy, meticulous and 'heroic' as Humboldt himself, though he rarely emerges from anonymity in Humboldt's *Relation historique.* Odd moments of danger reveal Bonpland's coolness; he saved Humboldt's life on the Orinoco when their boat capsized (Humboldt couldn't swim). He dissected crocodiles, howler monkeys and electric eels; when attacked by a runaway slave, he quickly recovered to pursue the slave through the prickly cactuses at Cumaná, and suffered headaches for weeks. Humboldt and Bonpland were passionate Republicans, and devoted to science. But Bonpland was not rich, nor well-connected, and unlike the asexual Humboldt he chased women, and ran off for a while at Angostura with an Indian girl.

Back in Paris from 1804 Humboldt lost his considerable fortune publishing the 30 volumes dedicated to his journey, not completed until 1835. This costly publishing venture alerted the curious reading public to the incredible scope of Humboldt's researches, and turned him into a celebrity. Generously Humboldt included Bonpland's name on every volume, so that he too became a household name. For example, Bonpland was originally meant to have written up the botanical discoveries, but the *Nova Genera et Species Plantarum* was delegated to W. Kunth who took 22 years to complete the volume. This impatience with indoor life and the methodical drudgery of writing tells us about Bonpland's yearning for adventures in the wild. In a letter to his brother soon after their arrival at Cumaná (in today's Venezuela) Humboldt wrote about the thrills of being in the New World: 'Bonpland assured me that he would go stark mad if the excitement didn't stop soon.' By 1810 Humboldt was begging Bonpland to work harder on the manuscripts for 'the high importance of science, for your own reputation, and for what you agreed with me in 1798'.

Up until 1816 Bonpland's life was a success story. He was born on the 28 August 1773 at La Rochelle, son of the chief surgeon in La Rochelle's hospital. His father's surname was Goujaud. Bonpland was an appropriate nickname for a future botanist. When Bonpland's father was born his father was tending vines and said: 'Dieu soit loué. Voici un bon plant' And it stuck. In 1791 he was in Paris studying anatomy In 1794 he joined the navy, but was back in Paris a year later studying zoology and botany with Lamarck and Jussieu. In August 1808, after the five-year South American trip, Bonpland was appointed botanist (really head gardener) at Empress Joséphine's Malmaison, helping her lay out the garden. He wrote a *Description des Plantes rares Cultivées à Malmaison et à Navarre,* 1813–1817 (with 54 colour plates made by Redouté). In 1810 he met a 24-year-old widow, one of Joséphine's childhood friends, married her in 1813, and lived to regret it. After attending Joséphine's funeral (she died on the 24 May 1814) Bonpland resigned from his post at Malmaison.

During these busy days back in France Bonpland cultivated close friendships with several Spanish American revolutionaries, especially Bolívar. Bonpland yearned to return to South America, and the nascent Republican states. In London (in Grafton Street) he met the Argentine radical Bernardino Rivadavia, who invited Bonpland out to found the Natural History Museum in Buenos Aires. From Bonpland's fateful acceptance in 1816 to his obscure death in 1858 he was tested in a Job-like manner.

Bonpland set out in the 200-ton mail boat the *Saint-Victor* from Le Havre on the 23 November 1816, and arrived at Buenos Aires, then a small capital of 35,000 inhabitants, on the 29 January 1817 (some 67 days). The same sea journey in 1976 took us 9 days from Genoa. You can fly direct from Heathrow in just over 11 hours. The distance, and time taken, suggest that Bonpland had left Europe for good. In fact he brought over 2,000 plants (over 40 varieties of orange and lemon trees), millions of seeds, and his precious South American herbarium, as well as his piano-playing French wife Adeline, and his step-daughter Emma. When they arrived in muddy Buenos Aires, with savage Indians in control of the pampas, no-one was expecting them. For a year Bonpland lived from selling vegetables and fruit from a market garden loaned to him at Hueco de los Sauces, today the plaza 24 de Noviembre. In 1818 he was officially appointed to his post, but without pay, and without a building. The struggle for power absorbed all Argentina's attentions. To survive, Bonpland allied himself with French merchants, nearly getting himself executed when some turned out to be conspirators.

As soon as he could he left Buenos Aires, obsessed by the possibility of exploiting *yerba maté,* the green, bitter tea rich in caffeine and vitamin C that today is the national drink outside the capital. He wrongly sensed its commercial potential; that it would replace China tea in Europe. The Jesuits had discovered the secrets of the *ilex para-guariensis* but after their expulsion from South America in 1767 all their beautifully ordered plantations went wild. Bonpland slowly un-ravelled some of the secrets. For example, no-one knew how to propagate the seeds. On a boat trip to the granite island called Martín García in 1819 Bonpland found some young shoots, and realized that the seeds had to pass through the intestines of a bird before they would flower. Martín García, only recently opened after years of being a military prison, lies four hours by motor boat from Buenos Aires, but nobody knew Bonpland had been there, though there is a journal of his trip in a safe holding Bonpland's archives.

In 1820 Bonpland abandoned wife and daughter and set off for Corrientes, a riverine town near the confluence of the Paraguay and Paraná rivers. From there he went by horseback over the swamps of the Iberá to the disputed mission area today called Misiones. He set up house in the red sandstone ruins of a Jesuit mission at Santa Ana, just outside Posadas, working with several local caciques, or bosses. The area is fertile, subtropical, virtual jungle. However, Dr Francia, the absolute, bachelor ruler of Paraguay got wind of Bonpland's arrival, thought he might be a spy, and resented any competition for what he considered his monopoly (yerba maté), and on the 8th December 1821 400 soldiers (another account said a 'considerable' amount) crossed the wide river, slaughtered Bonpland's workers, and brought him back in chains.

He was placed under village arrest in El Cerrito, near Santa María, another Jesuit ruin in the interior of Paraguay, and allowed to wander in a radius of one league. He was forbidden to speak French, or to receive mail, or visitors. Incredibly, this Dr Francia, whose dream it was to make Paraguay self-sufficient by excluding all foreigners, kept Bonpland prisoner for nine years in Santa María. A further extra-ordinary detail is that Bonpland never tried to escape, and even enjoyed his imprisonment with a thriving business, hospital and sawmill, and numerous Indian mistresses. This complacency with destiny shocked Sir Richard Burton who wrote in 1870 that 'The old Republican seems to have been a poor-spirited soul, who would volun-tarily have returned to his prison quarters.' There are 20 odd reports from spies on his activities in the Asunción archives, though Bonpland was not allowed to visit the capital. Bonpland never knew that his disappearance caused an international scandal, with interventions from Canning, Humboldt, Dom Pedro, Brazilian emperor, and a long letter Bolívar sent to Dr Francia threatening invasion if Bonpland was not released. All this hue and cry, and Bonpland told the English merchant John Parish Robertson that he regretted not being able to return to Paraguay. Then, just as capriciously, Francia decided in May 1829 to throw Bonpland out of Paraguay. Bonpland later wrote to a French scientist friend: 'I was a rich planter when dictator Francia ordered me to suddenly leave my land where I employed over 45 people.' He had to wait twenty months in another town, Itapúa, before crossing the river in a boat in 1830, with just his shirt on. At least, that was the romantic version; in fact he took eight carts, and horses with him.

Dr Francia was a hypochondriac who had Bonpland send him herbal remedies for which Bonpland had become famous. As a botanist doctor Bonpland realized how rich the land was in Indian herbal lore, and quickly adapted his European knowledge to this area. Francia was also an amateur astronomist, and fellow-scientist, but he never designed to meet Bonpland. Dr Francia had the only library in Paraguay with over 300 volumes, hated monks and Spaniards, was terrified of being assassinated, punished anybody who stared at him, and was fastidious and frugal. When he had his fits, he cared nothing for killing, euphemistically renaming the torture chamber the 'chamber of truth'. He was an odd tyrant, fictionalized by the American novelist Edward Lucas White in *El Supremo. A Romance of the Great Dictator of Paraguay,* 1916, as 'one of the greatest men this world has ever produced'.

From his liberation in 1831 to his death Bonpland earned his living from farming. He acquired land in several places along the Uruguay river (San Borja, Santa Ana), and set off whenever he could on botanical expeditions. He survived by working for different factions in the continuous civil wars wracking Argentina. And for a third time he lost everything, at the battle of Pago Largo when the opposing side under General Echagüe defeated the governor of Corrientes and slit the throat of 800 prisoners, including Bonpland's workers, inexplicably allowing Bonpland to live, ruined again. Over the later years Bonpland worked as an arms dealer, supplier of military uniforms, spy and doctor, befriending many of the anti-Rosas leaders, especially General Urquiza whom he visited at his wonderful palace San José in Entre Ríos (now a museum, and where Urquiza was murdered in 1870), advising the general on plants. By the end of his life, with three children, he had settled near Paso de los Libres.

Humboldt's caring for Bonpland's fate after his release from captivity is moving. He wrote to François Guizot (25 May 1833), the French politician and historian, thanking him for having got Bonpland the Légion d'Honneur. He had managed to get Bonpland a pension of 3,000 francs a year from Napoleon by donating his herbarium to the Jardin des Plants, adding: 'I let my collection go to be useful to my friend. I now do not possess even a blade of grass, not one reminder of Chimborazo!' Humboldt wrote 28 letters in his appalling handwriting on yellowing, stiff paper to Bonpland between 1831 and 1858, all kept in the Bonpland archives in Buenos Aires. One of his letters took six years to find Bonpland. Bonpland's letters back are scattered about in Europe. In all of them he recalls how intimate they had been, and complains incessantly about wanting to return to Europe, about his bad luck, the continuous wars, the lack of paper, the absence of good books; he tells about his merino sheep, his 1,600 orange trees. He tries to persuade Humboldt to spend his old age on the banks of the river

Uruguay ('I'm convinced that cold climates are bad for old people'). On the 25 December 1853 he wrote 'Very dear Humboldt, I hold all the circumstances of your famous voyage vividly in my mind . . .', and affirms his 'indestructible friendship', joking that together they have reached 165 years old. He added: 'I regret that I am so old, and that I love the banks of the river Uruguay so much'. Humboldt is his best friend, and when he reads one of Humboldt's books he hears his voice (they hadn't seen each other for 40 years). His last letter to Humboldt is dated 7 June 1857, annotated by Humboldt in a margin with the comment that Bonpland still shows his 'soif de vivre'.

Every year Bonpland would take a boat down to Montevideo to collect his pension. He continued to send plants back to Paris, in 1832 sending 25 cases, until 1849. In 1852 the French Académie des Sciences wrote Bonpland a letter of congratulation as the 'first to investigate the culture of maté and to try and improve it in a scientific manner', with a hand-written note by Cuvier encouraging him to 'continue with the same zeal to enrich science'. Bonpland had described six varieties, naming one *Ilex humboldtiana*. He also wrote a practical guide on yerba maté husbandry for his friend the governor of Corrientes in 1854, in perfect Spanish, signing his name Amado, not Aimé. He was also the first European botanist (in 1820) to observe one of the marvels of the floral world, the giant water lily (its upturned leaves reach 7 feet in diameter) called by its later British discoverer Charles Waterton the 'Victoria Regia'. Bonpland knew it as 'Mais de l'eau' because its huge seeds could be grated into flour.

What was left of Bonpland's legacy of 41 years in South America? There is a long street in Buenos Aires called Bonpland, though pronounce it in French and nobody understands you. There is a well-kept safe in a small museum called the Domínguez pharmacological museum in the university's Medical faculty. A postgraduate student looks after the place, and let me finger through all they have on Bonpland, from the 28 letters from Humboldt, to long correspondence with South American revolutionaries, to meticulous drawings of beetles and butterflies, to many laconic travel journals. He left copious notes on the Jesuits, on Guaraní (which he spoke), and other Indian languages. There are diplomas, and a passport issued in 1832 that

describes him as a white 'naturalist' with brown eyes, grey beard and
hair, and measuring 1.66m, with a large nose. There are letters from
bastard sons, from Emma his step-daughter who recounts a miserable
life as an orphan, not having heard from her step-father in 16 years.
This collection was found in cases stacked in an attic in 1905 by a
grandson who wrote a thesis on Bonpland's medical diary, with entries
in French on cholera, tetanus, an asthma attack, a long difficult birth,
and a recommendation to use granadilla bark to prevent dysentery in
troops in 1851.

There were also articles and documents in the decaying Biblioteca
Nacional where blind Jorge Luis Borges had been director, and more
stuff in the grand library of the Argentine Scientific Association.
There I chatted with the sole librarian who complained that one room
had been sealed up because he had got a strange fungal disease by
handling the papers. I realized as I read about Bonpland that he was
rediscovered every ten or so years by a journalist or a scientist, but that
no proper study of his work and life had been carried out. The best
description of the man came from a French doctor friend who met
Bonpland in 1840 and wrote a short biography in 1864 describing him
as austere, doggedly truthful, deeply reticent, and contented, 'heureux
toujours du présent'.

Having exhausted the libraries and collections we took an overnight
bus to Corrientes, where Greene had set his novel *The Honorary
Consul* in 1973 after staying there for a few days. Corrientes lies 1,030
kilometres upriver from Buenos Aires, and the orange tree-lined
streets were in reeking bloom. In 1854 Bonpland had been appointed
by the governor as first director of the Corrientes natural history
museum. Bonpland donated a duplicate of his plant collection of over
3,000 species. The museum still exists in the basement of a grand,
crumbly school. Inside there are fossil bones, geological maps and
specimen, and portraits of Bonpland and Humboldt. The woman in
charge hadn't a clue what had happened to Bonpland's plant collection. Here Bonpland is just a name. The Historical Museum also had
an oil painting of Bonpland (mis-spelt Bompland), a copy of a copy,
with his hair dyed black, and his top lip curling into a snarl. The
Director spotted us and introduced himself, he'd been to London

three times, had spent his own money restoring the house, and binding in leather the local archives. He warned me not to trust Argentine historians. Dr Hernán Bóo, a charmer, whose breath smelt of alcohol, and who had glaring memory blanks, knew some Bonpland descendants (one worked in a bank), some of the gossip, and put me right about Bonpland's supposed 'murder'. He also showed us a chest, and a chair where Bonpland had carved under the seat 'Amado Bonpland 1843'.

We took a nine-hour bus journey on to Posadas, capital of Misiones. In the nearby Jesuit ruins of Santa Ana Bonpland had established camp. Little is known of this site for no plans exist. A Spanish traveller, Felix de Azara, visited it just after the expulsion and mentions a large ornate church. By Bonpland's arrival 54 years later the scrub had taken over, the church had collapsed, leaving red stoned walls, and a large grass plaza. Nothing commemorates Bonpland. The neighbouring Jesuit ruins of San Ignacio (where the writer Horacio Quiroga lived his pioneer life, and whose self-built house is a small museum) are well-preseved, and famous.

Bonpland was taken across the river here into Paraguay. Today there is a bridge. In the parish records in Santa María , the other Jesuit ruins in Paraguay Bonpland was relegated to by dictator Francia, there are references to the birth of an Amado Bonpland; there's another table built by Bonpland, but nothing else has survived from his tranquil nine years as prisoner in this Indian red-earthed village. Itapúa where he spent a year is now a suburb of Encarnación, a noisy, smelly and dirty town. The bus we took was full of drunks, wobbled every time it gathered speed, and we sat next to a woman with a lamb on her lap. Everybody spoke Guaraní. Many writers from Voltaire to Sir Herbert Read, to Gordon Meyer, and recently Richard Gott ('models of utopian socialism') have lamented the expulsion of the Jesuits. The Jesuits had a printing press 80 years before one was set up in Buenos Aires, published their first book in 1703. They had tele-scopes in observatories, and in Candelaria, close to Santa Ana, a library of 4,725 books. The Jesuits wrote Guaraní dictionaries, imposed the Guarani language as a lingua franca (rather than Latin), and created a tradition of music and painting that had no rivalry in the

New World. They also cultivated *yerba maté*, originally known as
'Jesuit tea'. By Bonpland's time these missions were folk-memory, and
vegetation entangled ruins.

From Posadas we took a 12-hour bus journey across the state east to
Paso de los Libres on the Uruguay river, through red-dusty villages,
and acres of dwarf yerba maté plantations. In Paso de los Libres,
called Restauración in Bonpland's time, we hired a taxi to take us to
the village called Bonpland, hoping to locate his estancia or farm. The
village of Bonpland was built in 1927 as a railway station. The
intendente (local mayor) told us that the Bonpland family still owned
a farm 27 kilometres down river. We bumped along the sandy, dusty
road with yellow-flowered *espinillo* everywhere, but the forests of palm
trees have gone. We forded two streams as the chatty taxi driver
worried about his car. He knew nothing about Aimé Bonpland, and
had never asked himself what the name of the village meant. After
enquiring at two small farms, we reached 'El Recreo'. I walked over to
two men dressed in bombachas (baggy trousers tied at the ankle),
berets and ornate gaucho belts, drinking maté. One shyly introduced
himself as Juancho Bonpland, and told us how his great grandfather's
five square leagues of land had shrunk to 1,000 hectares. He touched a
huge casuarina tree, 'probably planted by Amado'. He pointed to an
old well 'always the first thing built on land'. The main house was a
bungalow with a tin roof, and verandah, in fact a shack. Inside on the
wall, to our shock, we were shown a convex glassed and framed repro-
duction of 'el sabio' (wise-man, scientist) Bonpland, with his daughter
Carmen next to him in another Victorian-framed portrait. All the time
this gaucho descendant had become more and more loquacious, hating
his English neighbours the Gibsons ('Los ingleses, qué hijos de puta').
He showed the room Bonpland died in, tiled, dirty, next to a primitive
kitchen. There was no electricity here, probably never will get it. The
shack had been built with wooden beams held together by leather
thongs as you couldn't get nails. This traditional man was deeply
proud of being a Bonpland, of his view on to the huge river Uruguay,
of his Argentine roots, a real *criollo*.

Back in Paso de los Libres we wandered into the cemetery, near a
shanty town. The taxi driver had warned us not to go there as it was

dangerous. We found Bonpland's tomb, completely abandoned. We could just make out the names Amado Bonpland and Encarnación Ramírez. The windows were smashed, the curtains dirty, no inscriptions on the urns inside. Bonpland of course was an atheist, though he became a mason late in his life. However, nearby there was a well-kept house-like family mausoleum, belonging to the Sánchez Bonplands, where Carmen, the daughter born in 1843 (when Bonpland was 70 years old) had died in 1928.

Bonpland had not been murdered. He had died naturally on his farm on the 11 May 1858, aged 85. The governor of the state of Corrientes, Juan Pujol, an admirer, had ordered that his body be embalmed by a Doctor Ribero. So it was taken the 27 kilometres from El Recreo to Paso, and embalmed. The doctor sat the embalmed body on a chair by an open door to dry out. A passing relation who was drunk, and resented Bonpland, shouted out something, and lost his temper when Bonpland ignored him. He pulled out his gaucho knife, a facón, and attacked the dead Bonpland. He so severely damaged the body that it had to be buried. That is how Bonpland was 'murdered'. The mausoleum promised to house Bonpland in Corrientes was never built.

An inventory of Bonpland's possessions after his death included 400 sheep, 7 pigs, 21 mules, 19 stallions, 200 horses, 14 cows, pears, fig, orange and peach trees, and listed his precious, dated, scientific books. He had died on his austere bed, made of leather stretched tight on a wooden frame. Bonpland's dream of publishing his formidable botanical journal never materialized until 1924 when a facsimile edition of one of his surviving botanical journals was published in Buenos Aires moving from entry number 2,450 in November 1849 to 2,884, December 1857. These entries are detailed in French, Latin and Spanish, but are dryly scientific, avoiding any mention of inner life. In 1854 he had written to Humboldt confessing: 'My sweetest hopes (I repeat this to you dear Humboldt) are to bring myself my collections and descriptions to Europe, familiarize myself with the latest works, the actual state of science, buy books, and as soon as possible return here to quietly await my end on the pleasant bank of the river Uruguay, surrounded by its splendid nature'. Bonpland had turned so native that he referred to himself with the Spanish Amado.

In 1974 the Paraguayan exiled novelist Roa Bastos revived Bonpland in his novel *Yo el supremo* (translated as *I the Supreme,* 1986). Roa Bastos invents a wise, relaxed doctor, secretly visited by dictator Francia. In footnotes he outlines Bonpland's life, including the letter from Bolívar offering to invade Paraguay, and has Bonpland 'murdered' by a Macario. In 1978 Bonpland's long South American life was turned into a 613 paged, documented novel *El solitario de Santa Ana* by Luis Gasula that also ends with the 'murder' of Bonpland's embalmed corpse, this time by a Diego Cristaldo. A recent novelized biography of Bonpland by Philippe Foucault, *Le pêcheur d'orchidées. Aimé Bonpland 1773–1858,* 1990, lifts Bonpland's 'murder' from Roa Bastos without saying so. Although Bonpland wrote little, and nothing about himself, his nomadic South American life surviving in turbulent times, awaits some magical realist. This could be his epitaph, from an 1848 letter: 'In spite of everything I am happy. Yes, dear friend, I am an old youthful and a happy man, living amongst flowers and loved ones. This marvellous America, full of contrasts, has bound me with strong ties.'

Gael Turnbull

BASS ROCK

With winds that are
so sheer they'd pry
the blue from the sky
and leave no scar.

Nikos Kavadias

A BLACK STOKER FROM DJIBOUTI

Willy, the stoker – a black from Djibouti –
whenever he'd finish an evening's work,
would come to my cabin, laughing, to tell me
fantastic stories. For hours he'd talk.

He told me they all smoke dope in Algiers;
in Aden they take white powder, and dance –
afterwards they shout, and talk to themselves,
dizzy, wrapped up in some weird trance.

He told how he'd seen himself one night, stoned,
on a white horse, galloping over the sea,
followed behind by mermaids with wings –
'Wait till we get to Aden – you'll see!'

I'd give him my sweets, and razor blades,
and warn him that dope can wipe out a man,
but always he'd only laugh again,
and lift me up in the air with one hand.

Such an innocent heart in so massive a body –
he saved me from trouble with some guy from Spain
one night in Marseilles; the Regina bar –
a bottle got smashed on his head for his pains.

We left him one day, dried up with fever,
out there in the East – body burning like tinder.
God of the blacks, forgive poor good Willy –
send him a little of that white powder.

Translated from the Greek by Simon Darragh.

Drummond
Allison

Drummond Allison, the fourth son of a well-off Chartered Accountant, was born in 1921 at Caterham. His mother was Austrian. Of the four brothers the eldest, who became a Headmaster, was eighteen years Drummond's senior; the second, fourteen years older, spent his life as a Forest Officer in Nigeria, and the third, a pilot in Bomber Command, was shot down over Wilhelmshaven in 1939. He was eight years older than Drummond.

At his preparatory school in Purley Allison rejoiced in the Arthurian Legends which influenced many of his later poems. He acquired a passion for cricket which he never lost. T. H. White, author of *The Once and Future King,* was a family friend who joined the Allisons on their annual Cornish holidays. Drummond was later to write an article on White in the Cherwell.

After Purley Allison went on a scholarship, to Bishop's Stortford College, surprisingly, since his three elder brothers all went to Caterham. Eric Jones, a contemporary of Allison's at Bishop's Stortford, wrote 'I got to know Ally, though he was two years younger, through the League of Nations Union. It was the time of the Peace Pledge Union . . . We read and discussed Left Wing Book Club publications: Spender's *Forward from Liberalism,* Orwell's *The Road to Wigan Pier,* and, above all Noel-Baker's *The Private Manufacture of Armaments.*'

Besides working on the school magazine Allison took part in school plays and became an enthusiastic choral singer.

In October 1939 Allison went up to Queen's College, Oxford. The pacifism of his schooldays was replaced by an acceptance of the war and he became a keen member of the OTC. Otherwise Oxford was mainly acting in Labour Club plays and writing for Cherwell.

In 1941 Michael Meyer edited an anthology called *Eight Oxford Poets,* whose star contributors were Keith Douglas, Sydney Keyes and

Drummond Allison. John Heath-Stubbs was another contributor who became a close friend.

Unlike many of his contemporaries Allison was able to complete his three years at Oxford, taking a 2nd class in Part 11 of the shortened Honour School of Modern History.

Allison's Oxford life was literary, political, social and dramatic. He had a large circle of friends, with whom he kept in touch as long as he was able.

By May 1942 Alison was at Sandhurst. He did further training in Plymouth and the Battle School in Northern Ireland. In 1943 he was on an Intelligence Course at Matlock. Robert Conquest, on the same course, described him as having a look of James Cagney. "'Sturdy' is the word I'd use for him."

Neither Conquest nor Allison shone in the eyes of the heavy-handed instructors, and were sent back to their regiments.

Allison had sent the MSS of a book of poems to the Fortune Press. It was to be called *The Yellow Night,* and proofs arrived just before he was seconded from the East Surreys to the West Surrey Regiment. He was sent almost immediately to North Africa and ordered to join the Queen's Own Royal Regiment, who had just relieved the Guards Brigade after heavy fighting on Monte Camino.

It was a cold, rainy autumn and conditions were almost as dangerous as the closely encamped Germans. Allison's platoon was instructed to make an assault on the German positions above them. Allison's CO described what happened in a letter to his parents:

'He was wounded leading his platoon in the attack on a German position at the top of the mountain and died a little later. I spoke to him myself as he was being carried down the mountainside by stretcher-bearers. He was very weak from loss of blood . . . He made a great effort, when he learned I was nearby, to speak and he managed in a whisper to tell me what was happening and what was necessary to silence the German machine gun which was holding up his platoon.'

Drummond Allison was buried in a Military Cemetery under Monte Camino. Both he and Sidney Keyes were killed within three weeks of going into action.

John Heath-Stubbs observed that 'Drummond was so much the

clown, lively and humourous, that we did not always take him
seriously enough as a poet. His poetry has in fact stood the test of time
better than that of Sidney Keyes.' Most critics would agree with that.

TWO UNPUBLISHED POEMS

WAR - POEM FOR ELAINE   April 1942

ing of pallor, running - coloured morning,
e night too poignant - starred, noon without meaning —
in my mind a slick prophetic play
ssantly, featuring: Death at bay,
e national figures ignorant of boundaries;
oes of laughter out of mines and foundries
ming the joyous noises - off, your heart
e Draper taking every part.
gleaming Bren-gun and in bayonet-shine
n eyes, behind the mortar bomb's high whine
tinctly your Welsh accents, may I find, and understand the
                                                    sign.

YOU GREAT AND GRUMBLING KINGS   April 1942

You great and grumbling Kings,
Weeping with wisdom are your speechless queens
Whose daughters tire of jewels in their teens,
Whose sons of softer things.

Those smiling merchants, who
Against rebellious barons now with loan
And foreign mercenaries hold your own
Obsequiously for you,

Will clutch at length the crown
That fable says fell from the friendly stars,
You will be proud to open slow bazaars
In an indifferent town.

And they themselves will see
Their markets and their trade-routes in the hand
Of the squat slave that bears your slanting brand
And breathes by your ~~august~~ decree.

The Collected Poems of Drummond Allison can be obtained from Stephen Benson, 10 Maze Green Road, Bishop's Stortford, Herts CM23 2QZ, price £9.99 plus £2 p&p (casebound).

Arturo Barea: Exile Without Resentment

When Arturo Barea reached England in March 1939, he was, in his own words, 'spiritually smashed . . . I disembarked with nothing. My life was broken in two. I had no perspectives, no country, no home, no job.' One of his stories, *Mr One,* written that same month expresses this mood. In it Barea describes two men, one a participant in World War One, the other a deserter. Both are ruined, emotionally and physically, by their experiences. In this nihilistic tale of two impossible choices, Barea was thinking of wasted lives in the final defeat of the Spanish Republic; recalling his own participation as well as his uneasy feeling that he had deserted. For he had left Spain before the war's end, abandoning his wife and four children.

Between Spain and England, Barea and his new wife Ilsa lived for a miserable year in a Parisian hotel, without even enough money to pay the bill and leave. They arrived in London penniless refugees. But not all was gloom for Barea in this 'midnight of the century'. After being 'buffeted from one side of Europe to the other', as he put it, he had found, unlike many of his less lucky compatriots, a safe haven. Moreover, he brought with him to England *The Forge*: and he sensed its value. He had destroyed the first draft because it was too abstract, very probably propagandistic like his book of stories, *Valor y Miedo* (Courage and Fear), published in Barcelona in 1938 and submerged in the war. For the second draft of *The Forge,* he had, in his own memorable words, . . . 'tried to wipe the slate of my mind clean of all reasoning and to go back to my beginnings, to things which I had smelled, seen, touched, and felt'.

But Barea's greatest fortune was that he was with the remarkable Ilse – or 'Ilsa' to him. Joan Gili, the Catalan publisher and translator, wrote of them: 'They complemented each other beautifully. She was

the brilliant intellectual and he was the intuitive eye of, say, *I am a camera* of Christopher Isherwood.'

Ilsa was an Austrian dissident Communist whom Barea had met at the height of the siege of Madrid in November 1936: she became his deputy in the Foreign Press Censorship. Bombarded daily from the front lines under two kilometres away, they both worked sixteen hours a day and slept on sofas in the office. The *Daily Express* journalist, Sefton Delmer, wrote vividly . . . 'Sandbags covered the windows. The chief [Barea] was a cadaverous Spaniard with deep furrows of bitterness around his mouth, dug deeper by the shadows from his candle.'

It was Ilsa's willpower that dragged a fatalistic and exhausted Arturo out of Spain. Without her, he would have stayed, in mental and physical collapse, most likely to become another statistic in the Civil War dead. She encouraged him to write. In turn, he nursed her through her own physical breakdown in Paris. For the rest of Barea's life they were to live in apparent harmony.

In September 1939, Tosco Fyvel met Barea and perceived in this melancholy figure a quality which was crucial to Barea's mental survival and development as a writer: a refusal to be dominated by resentment and his lack of bitterness despite his ordeals.

In some respects, Arturo Barea can be seen as the text-book exile: severed from his roots, always lonely and yearning for his lost country. Spanish critics tend to view him that way and there is evidence to support them. For example, he never learnt English properly: as late as 1956, when the BBC sent him to South America, his instructions had to be explained in Spanish. Secondly, for the last thirteen years of his life, he never missed the gossip from home in his weekly Friday lunches at the Majorca, a restaurant run by Spanish anarchists in Brewer Street, Soho.

As more weighty evidence for Barea's failure to put the past behind him, is the fact that he never wrote about anything other than Spain. And in his last novel, *The broken root* (1951), he showed that he had fallen into a trap fatal for exiles: he had lost touch with the realities of a changing society. In this book, Barea fails to imagine realistically a contemporary post-war Madrid and thus writes unconvincingly of an invented country.

But Barea should not be too rapidly pigeon-holed. In more important ways, Barea found his feet in exile. His very first article published in England, *A Spaniard in Hertfordshire,* indicated something of the role he was to adopt. This slight piece describes his pleasure at the unexpectedly kind and warm reception he and Ilsa had found in rural England. It was an England he had feared would be 'indifferent or hostile', for they had arrived bitter about British 'non-intervention' in the Civil War. But Barea rapidly made a distinction between people and government. This idea of unity of the peoples became the theme underlying the more than eight hundred fifteen-minute broadcasts he made for the BBC from 1940 onwards under the pseudonym of *Juan de Castilla.* There are weaknesses – of racial stereotyping and an oversweet view of the virtues of the English – in both this first article and the subsequent broadcasts. But his affectionate and often acute commentaries on England show he was by no means wholly wrapped up in Spanish affairs. Ilsa wrote just after his death: 'Perhaps he . . .

achieved what he hoped to do: to forge a link between this country, which he loved, and people of his own language overseas.'

Barea's adoption of British nationality in 1948 and his refusal to be drawn into the bickerings typical of exile life also suggest that he was not the archetypal lost soul forced to live abroad. But the clearest indications are in the sort of lives he and Ilsa led in England.

After staying from March to August 1939 in Puckeridge, Hertfordshire, the Bareas moved to Fladbury, near Evesham, when Ilsa got a job at the new BBC Monitoring Service. During the six war years she spent with the BBC, Ilsa's linguistic ability and mental speed made her one of the most valuable monitors. She not only listened to speeches by the German leaders and afterwards typed out a full text from her crude notes, but also monitored, often in poor reception conditions, broadcasts from Spain.

Margaret Rink, a colleague of Ilsa's, who lived with the Bareas at Fladbury, wrote: 'Arturo Barea was one of those people who are at home in any sort of company . . . He was tremendously popular in all the country pubs that were the "local" in whatever part of England he happened to be living.'

In the popular pubs his appalling mispronunciation of an English he had learned reading documents in his Madrid patents office did not appear to hinder his ability to (Margaret Rink again) . . . 'drink beer and play darts with the farm labourers, tease the landlord, and somehow, even when supplies were at their lowest, always manage to wangle from that gentleman a generous supply of beer, wine and cigarettes'.

Barea's personality allowed him to be more at home in the popular bars than in literary salons. Indeed, several people remember him as 'foul-mouthed', 'grumpy' or 'preferring his own company'. But others recall him as 'charming', 'the sort of man who would get into the front seat of a taxi in order to talk to the driver' or 'playful and mischievous, full of stories and jokes'. It depended who met him where. What is certain is that his overall lack of rancour and his relative integration into English life is intimately connected to the tremendous flowering of his literary talent between 1937 and 1944.

Before 1937, when he was 40 years old, Barea had written nothing.

Restlessly he had worked as a shop assistant, bank clerk, diamond buyer, company secretary, soldier, director of a toy factory and farm manager. He had had artistic yearnings, but had done no more than hang around literary salons and circus clowns for a few months. By the 1930s he had drifted into a remunerative but boring job as a patents agent.

The Spanish Civil War turned his life upside down. In eighteen months he ditched his mistress of six years, divorced the wife he didn't like and married a completely different sort of woman, Ilsa, an independent spirit who would certainly not put up with his shabby arrangements of previous years. In this same period, he became an important Communist Party-backed official of the Republican Government; was pressured out of this job for taking too independent a line; suffered a nervous breakdown after shell-shock; and just managed to leave the country on 22 February 1938, the day his exit visa expired.

Admidst this turmoil, he began to write: at first, sketches for the propaganda broadcasts he made from a mattress-muffled cellar as 'The Unknown Voice of Madrid'. By the time he left Spain, Barea knew he could become a writer. During the next six years, he had six books as well as several articles and stories published. He was a late starter, who had a lot to say about one subject. Once he'd said it, by 1944, that was it: he wrote little more.

The great qualities of the three volumes of *The forging of a rebel,* the finest Spanish testimony to come out of the Civil War, are Barea's honesty and passionate sincerity. He wrote *objectively* about himself. Barea's view of what was objective was not to weigh two points of view and come down in the middle. He believed in partisan involvement, thought you had to be involved to acquire objective knowledge. Thus he wrote what his senses told him. Horror and pleasures, charlatans and friends came alike to his unflinching eye: a camera eye, so direct and brutal at times that the reader is made to turn away. There is no distancing irony in Barea.

Peaceful Fladbury was the location for most of this writing on wars and revolution. There, among the vegetables and flowers, it was hard to believe that a war was raging in mainland Europe. For the first year,

Barea had little to do but . . . 'potter round . . . a large and very neglected garden' – and write.

The Bareas got to know a large number of people. There were the foreign intellectuals who worked with Ilsa: Martin Esslin, Isabel de Madariaga, Leonard Shapiro, Ernst Gombrich and the young George Weidenfeld, who remembers Barea's 'Inca face, finely chiselled, with deep-set eyes'. He certainly looked better than he had in the Civil War.

Fladbury was a multilingual, argumentative household, which the Bareas shared with Margaret Rink and Ilsa's elderly parents, who had caught 'the last train out of Vienna' before the war. Barea was the sort of cook who made huge, delicious *paellas* or chicken dishes to his own recipes but left heaps of washing-up, which he considered beneath his dignity to touch.

One of their many visitors was the elderly Sir Peter Chalmers-Mitchell, an ardent supporter of the Spanish Republic, who read and translated *The Forge* and had it accepted by Faber. Cyril Connolly came too and took away stories and articles for Horizon.

Barea's creative and bucolic life during this period was not without worry. Money was tight. Moreover, spectres of internment as an alien haunted him: going to London for an interview, he feared arrest.

He must, too, have suffered intense anxieties mixed with guilt about his family in Spain. His brother Miguel, 'Rafael' in the trilogy, was in prison and died in 1941/2 shortly after his release. Both his sister Concha, with seven children, and Aurelia, his ex-wife, with her and Barea's four, were living in poverty. And there was no way of making contact.

1941 was Barea's *annus mirabilis,* when both *The Forge* and *Struggle for the Spanish soul* were published. The former is his best book, a vivid evocation of life in the slums of Madrid and in nearby villages during the first years of the century. Barea's aim was to illuminate the social patterns which lay behind the Civil War. Through describing Barea's own childhood world, *The Forge* delineates the conditions which formed his generation.

Struggle was one of the *Searchlight* series and is a sophisticated dissection of the ideology used by Franco and of the historic forces on which the dictatorship based itself. The book is a corrective to those who have considered Barea only a naïf, spontaneous writer. Later that year, he started broadcasting weekly for the BBC Latin American service. Both artistically and economically, Barea was on his feet.

His first publication of 1941 had been an extended review of *For whom the bell tolls* in Horizon. When Hemingway's novel first came out, it had been the subject of protracted arguments round the dinner-table at Fladbury. There was a view that Hemingway was too important a friend of the Spanish Republic to be attacked. But Barea believed *For whom the bell tolls* was full of false notes. The guerrilla fighters behind the Nationalist lines were believable as hangers-on of the bullfight, but not as the Castilian peasants they were meant to be. He attacked Hemingway on the latter's own terrain – for lack of authenticity.

Barea used the article to develop his own idea of realism; not the propagandistic social realism of his own sketches in *Valor y Miedo*; nor what he called the 'dry, surface realism' of Pío Baroja, a precursor in writing about the Madrid working-class. Barea's objective was 'psychological realism', in which he aimed to delve below the surface and expose the 'hidden source of things'.

During the following two years, Barea completed the other two volumes of the trilogy, *The Track,* about the colonial war in Morocco in the 1920s, and *The Clash.* He also produced a beautifully written short book, *Lorca.* Visitors to Fladbury recall Barea reciting Lorca's poetry in his rasping voice.

Lorca is a polemical book. To understand the approach Barea took in this, his first sympathetic criticism, it is worth looking at the evolution of his attitude to other writers. He had been decidedly hostile to circles of writers and intellectuals since the age of sixteen, when the self-styled 'Last of the bohemians' Pedro de Répide had told him money could only be made in pornography. Barea had been disgusted by the acolytes who fawned on writers such as Benavente and Valle-Inclán in the cafés, and wanted no part of it.

He was more interested in the 'Free School' movement, one of whose offshoots was the famous 'Students' Residence' in Madrid, associated with one of the most brilliant artistic generations, including the poets, Lorca, Cernuda, Alberti and Aleixandre and also Dalí and Luis Buñuel. Remarkably, Barea was *never* to meet any of this, his own, literary generation.

He wrote: 'I was confronted with a new aristocracy . . . an aristocracy of the left . . . a very serious defect, the basic defect of all Spanish education: the doors were closed to working people.' He certainly never forgot his rebuffs. In his later critical essays Barea was wont to repeat that the Spanish people had two hungers: for food and for knowledge. And lack of knowledge kept them hungry.

But no writer can develop with crude hostility to all other writers; and during the Civil War, Barea began to like and respect some of the journalists and novelists he met. By the time he was living in Fladbury and himself becoming not only a creative writer but a literary critic, his attitude to intellectual circles had mellowed. Lord Weidenfeld recalls his turning up to BBC functions in slippers and ill-fitting clothes – but this can be attributed to playfulness, the assumption of a persona, just as when he grossly mispronounced English words, rather than any real hostility to the ambience.

In *Lorca,* Barea explains the poet's 'deep and lasting impression on the Spanish masses' by reference to his own experiences of reading and explaining Lorca to semi-literate militia-men he met in the war. Barea argues that, although Lorca never mentions politics, his imagery is so rooted in collective experience that he has a revolutionary impact. He made people feel and think.

Like everything Barea wrote, *Lorca* is thus a sort of addendum to his trilogy. It develops the twin aims Barea had set himself:

'I had a very personal objective: I wanted to discover how and why I became what I am . . . by calling up the images and sensations I had once seen and felt . . . I also had a general objective . . . to describe the shocks which had scarred my mind, because I am convinced that these shocks . . . scarred and shaped the minds of other Spaniards too.'

Lorca also contains an interesting discussion of exile. In New York, the poet . . . 'saw nothing but death and baseness in the city . . . Lorca, like so many others, refused to become part of a world other than his own, and thus that other world seemed to him only a living death.' But unlike Lorca, Barea's artistic vision was clarified by exile.

He understood Lorca's panic, but he did not share it.

In 1944, the Barea household followed Ilsa's job en bloc, when the Monitoring Service moved. They lived for two years at Rose Farm House, still a surprisingly remote spot by the Thames only a couple of miles outside Caversham. After a short time in Oxford, Arturo Barea's final home was at Middle Lodge, a house on the Fabian peer Lord Faringdon's estate, where he and Ilsa lived from June 1947.

At Faringdon, Barea continued to write, but with less intensity and volume. In these years he wrote *Unamuno* with Ilsa and his novel *The broken root,* as well as recomposing *The forging of a rebel* for its 1951 Buenos Aires publication, the first in Spanish. Ilsa and Arturo were both cavalier with their papers, which meant that Spanish versions had to be at least partially re-translated from the English versions because Barea's original manuscripts had been lost. This confusion has led to persistent rumours that Arturo Barea was not the author of *The forging of a rebel.* But there is plenty of evidence that he was, both internal, in idiosyncracies of style shared with *Valor y Miedo*; and external, in the testimonies of Olive Renier and Margaret Rink, who helped Ilsa with the English translations.

At Faringdon, Barea got to know a new generation, Ilsa's young Labour Party colleagues, and to them appeared a mellower, more relaxed figure. He liked to shoot pheasant, accompanied by his black dog, in Lord Faringdon's woods and enjoyed telling guests that he, a child of the Madrid slums, had entertained a genuine 'milord' on pheasant poached from his own woods (in fact, of course, shot with permission) and, to boot, the Lord had then done the washing-up. He frequented the local pubs, always looking for anecdotes for the apocryphal 'Six white elephants' of his broadcasts and enjoying effects such as asking for *bear* in the Wellington, Faringdon, on his return every Friday night from recording his weekly broadcast at Bush House.

For Ilsa these middle years of her life (she was born in 1902 on 20 August, the very same day five years after Arturo) were not easy. In Madrid Ilsa, with nearly two decades as a political organiser in Vienna behind her, had been 'highly intelligent' (Delmer); and 'feared' (Martha Gellhorn). A BBC colleague, Olive Renier, said: 'She was very dominating but good value . . . very serious . . . of sterling character, very brave, intelligent.'

Her translations of her husband's books are not only notable because she was translating from and into languages which were not her own, but rank with the very best of literary translations. She translated at least a dozen other books from both German and Spanish and worked as an interpreter. But life in post-war England for a clever, leftist foreign woman was harder than for her more gregarious husband. Ilsa was no habitué of popular pubs. She, too, did a few broadcasts, mainly for the Third Programme. But they petered out: her accent was too thick when she was nervous. And she was frequently ill, causing her to miss deadlines. Although she did not like to be known as Mrs Arturo Barea, inevitably she fell under her husband's shadow.

Ilsa's great achievement – apart from the translations – is her book *Vienna,* finally published after twenty years of on-off work in 1965. It is a social history of that city, interwoven with some of her family and childhood memories. Tantalisingly, it stops short after the First War, just when she herself joined the Communist movement, and so excludes any inside account of the events before and after February 1934. In 1968 she went back to live in Vienna for the first time in thirty-four years and died there in 1972.

Arturo Barea lived to enjoy some of the fruits of literary fame. He was invited to lecture at Pennsylvania State University for six months in 1952, a visit he had to cut short because the administration was under pressure for hiring 'reds'. He could not escape politics, though by this time he was no longer a socialist. Olive Renier wrote of a Majorca lunch with him in 1950: 'Arturo is deeply discouraged. He says that there is no hope anywhere. He sees no point in political activity because there is nothing you can say to people on any of the important matters which is true.'

The 1951 Buenos Aires publication of the trilogy brought Arturo Barea into touch with a Spanish-speaking audience for the first time. His apotheosis came in 1956, when he undertook a forty-nine-day visit, paid for by the BBC, to Uruguay, Chile and Argentina. For years *Juan de Castilla* had topped the annual poll as the BBC's most popular broadcaster to Latin America. On this visit, Barea was fêted on an emotional wave of sympathy and gratitude for his broadcasts and books.

Politics still pursued him: the Spanish embassies mobilised a counter-campaign, sneering at the 'English writer, Arturo Beria', referring to his acquired nationality and the supposed coincidence of his name and views with those of Stalin's henchman. In a tape that survives of a radio interview in Córdoba, Argentina, Barea emotionally expressed his gratitude at his reception and sounded a note which shows that however much he settled in England and took full advantage of life at Fladbury and Faringdon, he had not forgotten how his 'roots' had been severed: 'I feel my native country like a sharp pain. I never get used to it.'

In the afternoon of 24 December 1957, while Barea was pouring a whisky, he died suddenly of a heart attack in the presence of Ilsa and his sister Concha, who was seeing him again for the first time in twenty years. He was relatively young, sixty, but his heart had been weakened by the typhus he contracted when a soldier in Morocco. His books had to wait another twenty years, until after the dictator's death, to be published in Spain.

Daniel Pounds

TIBIA

Beneath the seven layers of the skin
The strength of an old and passionate love
Is hard like a shin-bone.

Hugo Williams

COME BACK TO STAY

As everyone knows by now,
Dickie and Rowland Soper
are travelling together
to Luxembourg,
where Dickie will be singing
Ireland's entry
in the Eurovision Song Contest,
with brother Rowland producing.
No one is predicting
just how successful
the lads will be,
but whatever the outcome,
one thing is certain,
back home in Ireland
'Come Back to Stay'
is sure to be one of the year's
biggest sellers
and a moneyspinner
for Rowland and Dickie.
So Good Luck to them!

A STAR IS BORN

Like most other showbands
The Hoedowners have had their
share of teething troubles
over the years.
The eponymous TV series
which should have re-launched
their ailing career
proved a mixed blessing.
Old wags shook their heads

and predicted the group
would be just another
bunch of also-rans
on the scrapheap of history.

All that has changed.
With their new disc release,
'Showball Crazy',
a bright new star had emerged
and taken his place
alongside the image idols.
His name is Sean Dunphy
and he is a natural.
Now even the knockers have to admit
the ex-carpenter from Co. Clare
has chipped his way
into the ranks
of musical greatness.

Jill Dawson

STOP AND SEARCH

Midnight and the police helicopter twirls its beam
over the city like the blade in a liquidiser

She's on the top floor, un-rolling a skein of hair
She hopes they're looking for her

Her hair falls, a jerky, auburn rope-ladder
down to the square. A drunk kicks

a milk bottle and shouts Fuck you Pigs
She knows they have new powers

and though she waits and even cries, once
Stop and search! why don't you? Despite

the force of her loneliness, which can transform
dead protein into this. Despite all that

no one climbs up to her

Judith Kazantzis

CALVES, CROSSING THE CHANNEL

In the ship's heart
a constant lowing,

tenor to tenor baritone, say,
among white iron,
under fluorescent strips.

On returning to my vehicle
I didn't expect this,

One rolling its eye,
heaving its head over the other's neck.
Like a daisy chain

we are all around
in our cars and caravans

like a long metal garland.

Claire Baines / At the Polish Café

Fall of a Prince

Christine Bernard was for a time my literary agent, and she told me an anecdote about Masud Khan that amazed and startled me at the time. Khan – a London psychotherapist – had been most helpful when I was seeking a publisher for a manuscript on Sylvia Plath, of which more later: he seemed, indeed, the one person in the world who understood what I was driving at, in applying recent theories from psychoanalysis to the criticism of modern literature. I knew that he was a close colleague of D. W. Winnicott, whose work had made such an impression upon me: he used to collect Winnicott after his day's work with patients, including children, and go home with him to transcribe and edit his case-notes and essays on psychoanalytical theory until the small hours. He was thus at the centre of an intellectual world to which I aspired to belong – one in which, as I believed, were emerging important insights into many problems of behaviour and meaning in our world.

Christine was a guest, one of five or six, at a dinner party Masud gave. Before, during and after dinner he was in a spiteful, witty, fretful mood and had been picking on the guests, one by one, particularly on a charming, gentle homosexual critic. As the evening passed Christine says she became increasingly nervous since he had not yet picked on her. After dinner the company returned to the drawing-room and Masud advanced towards her, drew up a chair and turned his searchlight attention on her. Ever sensitive to atmosphere, he must have sensed her fear and annoyance for he started to apologise for his earlier behaviour, his excuse being he was in a childish, 'roistering' mood. Christine replied, 'Surely, Masud, not so much roistering as *rude*.'

He stood up, and from his exceptional height glared down at her. 'No-one speaks to me like that! I'm afraid I must ask you to leave.' So she did. As did all the other guests: banished for *lèse majesté*! It was a way of behaving we just don't go in for, in the West.

Now it turns out that Khan's father, Rajah Khan, had four wives, and he was the second child of his father's fourth wife, Khursheed Begum, who was seventeen when his father married her at seventy-six. She was a beautiful, illiterate singing-and-dancing girl, a courtesan. In the extended family life of feudal Pakistan, his mother's origins were considered disgraceful and shameful. Pakistan society reveres motherhood and yet denigrates women: Khan played down his mother, although she was very much part of his sweetness and warmth and his seductiveness. Judy Cooper* suggests that his whole life was an acting out and search for his mother: while the only mother he found was later in Winnicott himself.

Yet this disgraceful and shameful background of his mother, and the isolation this provoked, meant that he could never resolve his relationship with women, and remained (as *The Times* called him in its obituary) a 'gifted outsider'. So, when a Western woman teased him

Speak to Me as I am: the Life and Work of Masud Khan (Karnak. £14.95).

and called his vanity in question, he would feel it dangerous enough to need to exclude and humiliate her, as he did Christine.

He must have had, obviously, a deep longing to be accepted, and this became manifest in the charm he could exert. He had a deep respect for the intellectual life and when he engaged with a topic it was done with love: he was rich in feeling and could have real sensitivity and compassion for another person. He was also extremely generous, in passing on psychoanalytical wisdom, as Judy Cooper makes clear. He had a penetrating capacity to use phenomenological disciplines, to understand the meanings of consciousness – as in his work on perversions. Yet he could be capable of outbursts of vituperative hostility, especially towards other psychotherapists. For example, he was once very scathing to me about R. D. Laing ('I saw Laing take the platform in what he chose to call the lotus position, with bare feet. Now the first thing you must be certain about in such a posture is that your *feet must be clean* . . .'). In the end, he became abusive and foul-mouthed, drank too much, played on snobbery, and became anti-semitic in a muslim way (though many of his friends in psychoanalysis were, of course, Jews). As Judy Cooper says, he had a problem with object constancy, and in the end he became grandiose, insisting on being called 'Prince': he seemed incapable of guilt, remorse or of wanting to be forgiven: the virtues of the depressive position, and of Western Christianity. Charles Rycroft called him 'the Damaged Archangel'. Judy Cooper treads a careful path, between recognition of Masud Khan as a colourful, charismatic and insightful figure, and a womanizer, snob, anti–Semite, in the end a self-destructive demon – recognising that some of the problems arose from his long and painful struggle with lung cancer. He became impossible in the end, and turned his rebellious and violent rage on the British Psychoanalytical Society, who struck him off in 1988. By then he had lost his voice completely, and was almost entirely cut off from the world. Because he was the author of so many much-admired books and papers, and had kept the green International Psychoanalytical Library flourishing, his fall into such a damnable end was much lamented. His affair with a patient finally ruined him within the British Psychoanalytical Society, whose journals he edited.

What attention ought we to give to the theories of such an impossible man? Judy Cooper asserts that, judging from her own analysis with him, he was an extremely gifted and sensitive clinician. Eric Rayner, a psychotherapist who writes a preface to this book, says 'He had a magical understanding of people and a feeling for them.' He was a 'charismatic' analyst, often authoritarian with the imperious manner of an Eastern potentate, but managed to combine this with tenderness and tolerance. Judy Cooper says she found in him the father she needed. In these maverick modes, being a law unto himself, there was both freedom and danger, and in the end the dangers destroyed him.

He was unique in his cross-fertilising interweaving of various theories especially from Freud, Fairbairn and Winnicott. At the centre of his attention was the way the self was formed, and the nature of the schizoid deficiencies in self-hood.

He was a real intellectual and displayed enormous erudition, and was familiar with many literary English and French writers. He also had a rich Eastern cultural background, both Persian and Sanskrit: as somebody says 'he knew about everything'. It is also true that he would intuitively dominate any room he was in, and took a natural lead in any group, as I found when he asked me to talk to the '52 Group of Psychoanalysts.

His consciousness was much influenced by his upbringing, and especially by the very different role of the mother in the East, where a woman's status as a mother is crucial. Cooper believes that Masud Khan was inhibited by his own problems from investigating this area of cultural division, around the role of the woman. He had acute problems with women analysts.

But coming from the East he was better able than westerners to tolerate madness, contradictions and unusual solutions (one of his patients found his way back to mobility and aliveness by roller-skating, accompanied by Masud Khan's houseboy). Some critics have also argued that in his hands psychoanalysis ended up as a branch of literary criticism, and this points to the origins of psychoanalysis itself not only in Vienna but in English literature itself, as a source of explanations of the internal world and as a source for a model of the mind. I was certainly startled (and gratified) when Masud Khan wrote to me, after reading the manuscript of my book on Sylvia Plath, 'I have no hesitation in saying that I have learned greatly from your book, not only about the meaning of idolised dismay in Sylvia Plath's poetry, but also in terms of my own clinical thinking.'

It is also worth recalling that he was very sympathetic to my doubtful analysis of much of twentieth-century western culture. 'The truth of the situation,' he said, 'is that in the contemporary European cultures there is an acute and profound dread of the pain of positive living . . . how right you are "the courage we require is the courage to be human", and in the hands of so-called extremist writers this "courage" has taken on the stance of the dissolution of that which is human. To cheat with dismay (Sylvia Plath), violence (Genet), dismembered eroticism (Burroughs), abreactive yet astringent mentation (Sartre), or socio-political nihilistic euphoria (Fanon and Cleaver) has become the signature of the verity of self-hood today, and most of the critics are the evangelists to this bizarre phenomenon . . .'

He was, incidentally, highly critical of my approach: 'you make no allowance for the instant-anxiousness of the self-styled intellectual revolutionaries of today, to whom language is not a vehicle for insight that promotes painful growth, but a conceptual game to keep themselves and others distracted'.

Judy Cooper admits Khan's brilliance as a therapist but suggests that one needs to be a little more boring, that is, grounded, stable and predictable, to be a good analyst. Khan's paternalism she sees as caretaking responsibility on the lines of an Eastern patriarch. Some of his case-histories, she suggests, if not fiction, were elaborately embroidered for dramatic effect. In practice he was often unpredictable, sometimes being bored and irritated, and not wanting to talk about anything: he would change times and cancel sessions. But Judy Cooper records her considerable indebtedness, not least in her own work as therapist.

Khan did both bad and good work, both with patients and in his writings. He would stir up tremendous anger in some people, and met a murky end at the hands of his colleagues. But he was admired and revered as a distinguished contributor to the international world of psychoanalysis. He was both honest and deceitful: creative and destructive, loving and cruel. He was a misfit both in the East and in London, a talented, lonely and tormented man. He had a touch of genius, but referred to himself as 'a looked-down-upon peasant'.

Some of us have glimpsed in the findings of psychotherapy new sources of values — in the very way between them, therapists and their clients search for authenticity and existential meaning, in mutual trust and in distrust of all authoritarian solutions. From this point of view, many manifestations, such as the obsession with sex in today's culture, or the idolisation of perversion, seem shams, belonging to false solutions (I used Masud Khan's insights in detail in *Sex and Dehumanization*). It is a terrible shock to find that certain leading therapists, such as Lacan, R. D. Laing, and Masud Khan, can also be such terrible people, often directing a demonic destructiveness against the creative dynamics of psychoanalysis itself, and doing the movement immense harm, not least by offering enemies a seeming justification for dismissing the whole discipline. (At least Winnicott was never capable of such lapses.) Judy Cooper's sympathetic book, written in tribute to Masud Khan's best contributions, but without attempting to hide his more outrageous side, will help us to come to terms with the disaster to psychoanalysis that Prince Masud Khan's fall was.

Peter Bakowski

BATH PLUG

A way
to edit
water.

CARVE, CARVE THE LAKE

Only the swan
is lonelier
than the
shop window mannequin.

Lawrence Sail

HOMAGE TO PAUL KLEE

Alphabet Country

And now you are entering
Alphabet country
You may look to lodge by the red road
In Villa R. The rates are reasonable,
The food adequate, instruction free.

In general, do not
Ask too many questions.
Y, by the way, is a gulf or bird,
Also the shapes of trees in a park
Near L (Lucerne is one suggestion).

You'll soon learn the logic
Of literal vision –
C, of course, for a ship in harbour,
H for father, thus I for mother,
While B gives birth to a composition.

Some meanings, though,
Can never be amended –
W is always woe, branded
On the child's brow: Mister Z,
Grim bossman, is hardly a friend.

Above all, beware
When letters attempt
To get together. Such combinations
Are IRR (quite mad) or RIP,
Perverse analysis (is that all it meant?).

The best you can hope for
Is a four-letter code.
Example: when L is not Lucerne
It could be Lily at the piano, playing
Bach in love's authentic mode.

Other examples:
Paul, or still better
Klee — a four-leafed German clover,
A French key and an English reminder
Of N on a headstone, the final dead letter.

Connie Bensley

MOLLUSCULAR ROMANCE

The octopus has many arms —
   I'd like to know if you
   wish I had too.

The octopus turns white when shocked
   and I'd turn white and grieve
   if you should leave.

The octopus has got three hearts
   but I had only one
   and now have none.

Christine McNeill

VIENNESE STILL LIFE

This gallery has been his ground
of natural limits. From the radiator
he ruminates on Spinoza's theory:
whether short- or far-sighted
one can break the light.

The Japanese walk in
as into an eating bowl.
Searching behind the varnish
for something more than paint.
The walls are full of limbs.

In 1940 he was a bomber pilot.
At night he played God with 'Christmas
trees'; flares that he threw down
to illuminate a town or village
before attacking it.

The floor creaks.
The Japanese bow
before the pictures' signatures.
Art, to him, is a mixed marriage of trees.
Pink and clean, the bodies belong to no one.

Michael Pearson, East Coasting

Michael Pearson

Christopher Wren

THE MAYA WENT DOWN TO ZERO

I can no longer tell the difference
    between the sound of jangling keys
and the songs of indignant starlings.

I can no longer unfold your letters
    without tremors along my lips
and chattering between my teeth.

I can no longer accept the warning
    'you will die before your time'
as a valid concern for us here.

I can no longer look for Venus
    the star of the mornings and evenings
without marvelling at the Maya.

Once upon a very long time ago
    the Maya took numbers beyond one
and out of nothing they created zero.

I have made a Maya diary to use
    with 584 days in the year:
the time Venus takes to orbit the earth.

Zero is the twenty-seventh day
    of May nineteen ninety one
I leave prison on their new year's eve.

One day I'll be looking starwards
    and see Venus through the sky of Milos
perhaps then I'll not want to die.

('Were her one and a half arms broken there?'
    You wondered in your last letter.
They've searched the ruins and bays in vain).

Yes, I'll set sail for the isle of Milos
    and examine the songs of starlings
without the keys and their janglings.

Martyn Crucefix

SOME FIRST STEPS

Gravel bit like scissors into my knee.
Flesh opened with a pouting lower lip,
bled quickly at the rim, white at the root.

She planted me high on a stool at the sink
and bathed the wound, bending low
to pick tiny stones like shrapnel from it.
It hurt like cheese-wire noosed round
trembling bone. So I locked my gaze
to the lowered crown of her mousey head,
to the thick hair's shell-like spiral.

But as the pain began to uncoil,
as she murmured *my little wounded man,*
as she massaged my leg till it burned,
my gaze slipped to where her dress fell loose,
down the receding, egg-freckled, trembling gorge.

FRANK McGUINNESS

The Plays of Brian Friel

First a question to chafe the Anglo-Saxon conscience 'What happens whan a small nation that has been manipulated and abused for hundreds of years by a huge colonial power wrests its freedom by blood and anguish?' A somewhat euphemistic variation on an old plaint, you might say, more rhetorical than inquisitive, and – no prizes for identifying *which* 'small nation' – generally a signal in Hibernian circles for a barrage of rebel songs all brayed to the same dismal tune. Yes, we are back in the could country.

In fact, the words belong to a character in Brian Friel's *The Munday Scheme,* which plots the attempt of an unhinged and corrupt taoisach to sell off the west of Ireland as an international cemetery. An early work, it promises more than it delivers, eventually petering out in a splutter of moral indignation that invariably spells death to comic inventiveness. Nevertheless, it not only raises the question of post-colonial Ireland, but even dares, the Lord have mercy on us, to be satirical about the matter, something to raise a cheer among those few brave hearts weary of Kevin Barry and the shop-soiled 'terrible beauty' that has effectively licensed gangsterism on both sides of the border for the last seventy years. Not that this will make a scrap of difference in a country whose writers for the most part seem content to remain slumped in habitual and bibulous contemplation of their ancient myths and legends, some of which, the more cynical might murmur, stretch back as far as 1916. No. We may be sure that even to the fourth and fifth generation, in such far-flung outposts as Boston, Liverpool and Sydney, occupied by the Irish for the institution of Easter Duties and the rhythm method, the sons and daughters of Erin, still anguished if not actually bloodied, will continue to crack on about the martyrdom they have endured. Even worse, they will continue to pump out gimcrack imitations of *The Playboy* and *Juno* that might have been fashioned out of DIY kits. Nothing could be easier, if the following simple instructions are followed. (1) lard your dialogue with enough emphatic personal pronouns to suggest Synge *himself* might have penned it; (2) remember that – if you're after winning the plaudits of the critics for your fine command of the Anglo-Irish idiom – *after* takes not the perfect, but the present tense; (3) embellish the assembled article with sufficient effulgent imagery to ensure that it will have been hailed as a darling of a play before the second glass of porter has been supped at the theatre bar.

Lest I should be misunderstood, I should at once point out that these strictures, though they stem from something he wrote, probably apply less to Friel than any other Irish playwright of the last twenty or thirty years. The fact is that if we accept Beckett as a maverick talent gone native among those absurd, not to say cruel, Europeans, and Behan, in spite of one good play and a near miss, as a largely unfulfilled potential, he remains the only Irish dramatist who genuinely measures up to Synge and O'Casey, even to the extent of having had a play rejected by the Abbey.

His affinity with Synge may be considered particularly marked. He shares with the older writer a profound affection for the west of Ireland and its people, although, as a product of peasant stock himself, perhaps slighly less credulous than the cultivated and cosmopolitan chronicler of *The Aran Islands,* who – shades of Orwell – never fully understood the alien culture in which he chose to live. This was, as Friel would know from his own childhood, much of it spent in Donegal, a way of life that had scarcely changed in generations and was light years away from even the urban bustle of Dublin, never mind England and America. This has, of course, become less and less true as the levelling process of modern communication has taken its effect, something Friel vehemently regrets, lamenting the loss of so many traditional Irish customs as the country fast becomes a tawdry extension of America. This is not to cast him as some sort of literary Luddite, a sentimentalist seeking to preserve a life-style because he thinks it quaint or picturesque. Such an adjuration would be about as substantial as a pop singer's concern for the Third World. The truth is that no one has written with more compassion and insight about the crumbling and defeated environs of the west of Ireland, a fact amply demonstrated in such powerful works as *Philadelphia, Here I Come!, The Gentle Island, Translations* and *Dancing at Lughnasa*. If he mourns some aspects of a dying culture, the reduction of a rich local dialect to the homogenised accents of television, say, he blinks none of the hard facts and choices his characters face.

A glance at a catalogue of Friel's works leaves one slightly overwhelmed by how much he has written. Starting out as a short story writer, he had already established a considerable repution when he turned to drama, learning his new craft by writing for radio and television. Recollection of these early plays such as *A Sort of Freedom* and *To This Hard House* show how clearly they adumbrated the path he was to take as a dramatist and the preoccupations that were to absorb him. For the most part, this was about the business of scratching a living in a depressed community, a prospectus usually centred on one family and the relationships, frequently brutal and unforgiving, within it. In particular, he was fascinated by what went on between fathers and sons in a society that eschewed any show of affection between men, a constraint often leaving them as emotionally crippled as their mothers and wives were patient and resigned. Traditional Irish themes, in short, to which he soon added another, emigration and the dilemma it poses for the poor, particularly the young, in societies which have little to offer them. The grief often accompanying the decision to emigrate is movingly captured in the play that probably first alerted us to the fact that a significant new talent had appeared on the scene. *Philadelphia, Here I Come!* covers the final hours Gareth O'Donnell spends in his father's house in Ballybeg – a fictitious Donegal village, a microcosm of Ireland, in which Friel has set a number of his works – before his departure for America. He is wracked with doubt and remorse, his torment finally exploding in a yell of defiance which only reveals what is troubling him even as it attempts to buttress his

resolve: 'All this bloody yap about father and son and all this senti-
mental rubbish about "homeland" and "birthplace" – Yap! Bloody yap!
Impermanence – anonymity – that's what I'm looking for; a vast restless place that doesn't give a damn about the past.' Behind these brave
words, however, lurks the dread that the anonymity sought will add up
to no more than 'one bloody room in Kilburn', the future forecast for
another would-be exile in the ironically titled *A Gentle Island*. But
even this may not be the ultimate humiliation, a lesson bleakly illustrated in *The Loves of Cass McGuire,* the brash but essentially warm-
hearted migrant of the title returning from the States after fifty years
only to find she has become an embarrassment to her upwardly mobile
family and a candidate for an old folks' home, the cost being met, the
final irony, from the accumulated dollars she has skimped to send back
over the years, unaware that those she left behind were on the up.

Friel's plays confront sombre social issues, but it should not be
assumed that they are turgid and solemn in the way of so many *serious*
works. Not a bit of it. A dramatist as opposed to a social commentator,
he is more concerned with the fluctuating inter-play among his
characters than with the backcloth against which they move, acutely
observed though this may be. Thus in *Philadelphia,* the dire economic
circumstances that prompt Gar's emigration are less vividly recalled
than his relationship with his father, the acheing, unacknowledged
love they have for each other, never articulated, and yet, as if by some
theatrical osmosis, marvellously conveyed in their fierce exchanges
and apparent contempt for each other. It is an illustration of Friel's
rare gift for revealing more by what he leaves unsaid than by what is
clearly enunciated, a talent never more subtly demonstrated than in
the gentle, funny, nostalgic and finally heart-acheing *Dancing at
Lughnasa,* a tale of five sisters in which little or nothing happens, but
which resonates throughout with the concealed passion, hope, despair,
jealousy, and Lord knows what else, behind the chitchat and amiable
façade of a cosy family group. It reminds one of Chekhov, a writer
Friel admires and whose *Three Sisters* he brilliantly transcribed into
English – or Irish as he would probably have it, insisting as he does
that the languages are different, which, let's face it, may come as an
eye-opener to a Kerryman seeking work in Birkenhead.

When asked how the people of Aran who had known only toil and deprivation could still prove so ebulliently comic and eloquent, Synge observed: '. . . it is only in wild jest and laughter that they can express their lonelines and desolation.' This finds an echo in Friel's *Translations,* when Hugh, a polyglot teacher in a hedge-school, quizzed by an Englishman about the opulence of the Irish language, comments: 'It is our response to mud cabins and a diet of potatoes; our only method of replying to . . . inevitabilities.'

The play is set at the time of the ordinance survey conducted by the military in 1824 and the shattering effect it had on the Irish and their native tongue as traditional place names were anglicised. It is a subject that Friel was clearly drawn to by the curious value he himself attaches to place names. This goes much deeper than his obvious pleasures in the supple and meandering diction of the west coast, a dialect he renders as exactly as Synge and, moreover, guiltless of embroidering for poetic effect. It is almost as if language – and place names particularly as they foster a strong sense of the locale – is invested with some magical property which holds the key to the racial memory in which he believes. It is, presumably, something akin to what John Montague is driving at when he writes:

'This whole landscape is a manuscript
We had lost the skill to read
A part of our past disinherited.'

Certainly, it is a belief which the hedge-schoolmaster would appear ready to swallow when he opines: 'It is not the literal past, the *facts* of history that shape us, but images of the past embodied in language.' For my few punts, however, this would seem a trip back into the Celtic twilight zone and one can only guess at the reaction of such revisionist historians as R. F. Foster, committed as they are to demythologising Irish history and substituting a few legends with a fact or two. Not that academics would seem to cut much ice with Friel as is evidenced by the short shrift given Tom, an historian we encounter in *Aristocrats,* the playwright's perceptive look at a strangely neglected stratum of Irish society, the Catholic upper class. Tom, an American, is researching the history of the family, an enterprise which finds little favour with Eamon, the quintessential magniloquent Irish romantic, who remarks: 'There are certain things, certain truths that are beyond Tom's kind of scrutiny.'

I must confess to a distinct unease when I hear scholarship rejected in favour of instinct and mystical understanding. Dangerous bogland, perhaps, and a landscape to remind us of another of Montague's lines when he speaks of 'the vomit surge of race hatred' inherited from his father. Powerful stuff, but a bequest denied many of us, whatever else we might blame on the ould fella.

At the same time there is no denying that Friel exploits his pre-occupation with names to stunning effect, notably in the scene when his star-crossed lovers, an English officer and an Irish peasant girl, sharing no language, begin to communicate with each other by mouthing the place names in each other's background, a recital that slowly swells into a crooning love duet. He also employs it with graphic force in his extraordinary *Faith Healer* in which Frank, a some-what improbable shaman, is much given to reciting a litany of Welsh place names, 'just for the mesmerism, the sedation of the incantation'.

No more than a succession of four monologues, *Faith Healer* reminds us that Friel has never been afraid to experiment, not always with the approval of the critics. No surprise there. What may be revered as *verfremdungseffekt* when employed by a German Marxist can rapidly become failure of stage technique in other hands. The fact is that if some of his innovations have been less than totally successful – a surfeit of tricksiness in *The Loves of Cass McGuire,* for example – the notion of representing both the private and public aspects of Gar O'Donnell's persona, his alter ego being played by another actor, paid off. Equally successful was the decision to have the adult narrator in *Dancing at Lughnasa* play himself as a child, thereby not only freeing the playwright from the shackles of sequential time, but also dis-tancing us from the action as if it were something remembered.

Although plays like *Volunteers* confront political issues – the play is about a group of IRA prisoners who volunteer, against orders and thus risk execution, to help in an archaeological dig – Friel is not a political playwright in the sense that he has some message or is writing to a manifesto. This is true of even his most overtly political work, *Freedom of the City,* which was obviously inspired by the events of Bloody Sunday. It was, admittedly, written from a republican view-point – although, let me quickly add, this does not necessarily vitiate the truth of what it portrays – but even so, it is difficult to comprehend why the London production should have roused such hostility. It may be, of course, that this was a reaction to Friel's public declaration of himself as a republican who does not accept the legitimacy of the border and wants the Brits out. This strikes me as his business and about as relevant to his work as his collar size, although David Hare, I suspect, still smarting from the drubbing given his latest play on the strength of everything but its merits as an actual drama, would probably think such a conclusion disingenuous. Nor should we forget that not even George Orwell himself was above accusing O'Casey of nationalistic prejudice. No matter. *Freedom of the City* may be no great shakes as a play, but what this story of three civil rights marchers gunned down by the army does give us is the paradoxical and contradictory flavour of Irish politics, something which the English have never fully fathomed. One sympathises with them. It is difficult to equate the nauseating sentimentality of those instant ballads with, say, the debunking and irreverent graffito: 'We'll never forget you Jimmy Sands'.

   The setting of Friel's latest work, *Wonderful Tennessee,** is a derelict jetty on the Donegal coast, a vantage point offering fleeting glimpses of the mysterious island, *Oilean Draiochta.* Steeped in legend and once the home of a monastic order and a mecca for pilgrims seeking cures, it has now long since been abandoned. The calm that surrounds it, however, is soon to be broken by the arrival of a jubilant birthday party, three couples, their lives inextricably bound by ties of matrimony, kinship and affection. Silver-tongued and sophisticated town-dwellers, their plan to visit the enchanted isle is frustrated by the non-arrival of the boatman, the eternally procrastinating Irish peasant, 'ancient; and filthy; and toothless. And bloody smiling all the time.' They wait, supping champagne and nibbling the odd Romanian truffle or brandied peach, filling the long hours with stories and songs, old,

*Faber. £5.99

new, sacred and profane. The mood of the revelry slowly subsides, however, and a more sombre tone becomes evident as we begin to detect the bitterness, disappointment, hurt and duplicity that lie behind the routine joshing and easy camaraderie. All have something to hide, be it the disturbed Berna lamenting her childless and empty marriage with the chillingly desolate confession, 'There are times when I feel I'm . . . about to be happy', or the desperate Trish, tensely protective of her dying husband, but consumed with the guilt of having destroyed his concert career by forcing him to fill a more lucrative spot in her brother's pop group. Then there is Frank, his inadequacy cloaked in wise-cracking and erudite banter, the time-honoured refuge of failed Irish romantics. Yet it is he, the arch-sceptic when the question of apparitions is raised, who first senses the magic in the air about them, the feeling that like the departed medieval monks possessed with 'a rage for the absolute', they might almost be in touch with 'what is beyond language. The inexpressible. The ineffable.' It is something of which they all become aware to some extent, the play ending on a ritualistic note as they bedeck a rotting lifebelt post with articles of clothing, an echo of the pilgrimage undertaken by Terry and his father many years before.

If this is to make the play sound fey, it reckons without Friel's robust humour and the brilliance with which he constructs characters and establishes the chemistry that exists between them. The play is a marvel of shifting moods, at one moment gay and sparkling, the next charged with danger and the fear that something is about to occur that will destroy the fragile equilibrium of the group forever. As in *Dancing at Lughnasa,* nothing much appears to happen, but the gradual revelation of the dark secrets of the bunch, accomplished almost by sleight of hand, once again confirms Friel as a playwright of the first order.

Paul Munden

RETRIEVER

Something snappy was the brief.
All that came to mind

was how your cancer-riddled bone broke
open, light as an *Aero* bar.

*

The pale pink rims of your eyes
were disquieting but we were told

*They're often like that
if there's chocolate in the litter.*

CASTERBRIDGE

She fell for the period atmosphere
of a town she knew and, when the series ended,
told me she'd lost a friend.

The rubbish in the streets was to cover
the yellow NO PARKING lines
I said, compounding her loss.

Deryn Rees-Jones

THE GREAT MUTANDO

Pulls rabbits out of hats
Ties up the day with handkerchiefs in silk.

So many colours make me cry.
LADIES AND GENTLEMEN, FOR MY NEXT TRICK!

He spins the earth.
Blues. Greens. A plate

On a stick.
Punch. Judy.

Five silver glistening rings.
That link

Then come apart.
Six doves.

Five fly, one suffocates.
A little drop of shit runs down his sleeve.

He makes a Dachshund from three pink balloons
Mutando!

I want a name like that.
And a world.

Wands. Fairy Godmothers.
No crocodiles.

A place where I can get the handkerchiefs to knot.

Beatrice Garland

NOCTURNE

My serious friend, one winter day you brought
me Chopin nocturnes played by Ashkenazy —
limpid, elegant, more than anything about
the transient, the casual felicity
of particular events: how one summer a woman
sewing on a terrace might lift her head
to meet the gaze of the dark-haired man
who arrived unannounced that day. Nothing is said.
Her hands rest on her lap. And the valley might deepen
to black, the pipistrelles flicker past
the golden squares of the windows, like now, open
to the warm night, the music, the quiet guest.

RELATIVITY

Wild carrot flowers
float above the field
on invisible stalks:
half a million stars
in an upside-down soft
green tussocky sky.

Upholstered in chenille,
fat orange moths
veer erratically among
the knee-high galaxies,
with messages, provisions,
toted from star to star.

From high up on the hill
I watch you, terrestrial man,
putting your bags in the car.
This event took place
light years away.
Still, I wave goodbye.

Frances Nagle

LOVER

If I look
From my bedroom
I can almost see your house;

Your children –
Count them through their birthdays;
Setting out;

Your wife –
A naked blur
Behind the bathroom window;

And you,
Across the bed,
Or putting your clothes on briskly,

Your watch,
Her present,
Snapping against your skin.

Siberia

KENNETH MEYER

Atop The Black Dragon

Captain Xue stood at the southern terminus of the bridge spanning the dark river and looked across at the Russian officer and his enlisted man at the wooden guardhouse opposite them. Xue and today's guard both wore green People's Liberation Army overcoats, heavily-padded against the northern cold, and matching Manchurian lined hats with the long earflaps. Xue of course also had an officer's green cloth cap with black brim, but wasn't so insane as to wish to wear it on a day like today. The gold buttons on the PLA men's overcoats gleamed in the noonday sun.

Across the river, the Russians wore heavy grey overcoats of the same style and even the same Manchurian-style hats. Xue couldn't remember what colour the Russian buttons were. The two contingents of guards faced each other across the river.

The name of the place was Mohe, and Xue and his comrades derived great amusement from this name, being as it was a pun on the Chinese word for 'somewhere' or 'something'. Mohe was a small town along the Black Dragon River, which formed the border between Russia's Siberia and the Chinese province of Heilongjiang ('Black Dragon River'). Mohe was one of the northernmost points in the province. Captain Xue and his comrades would ask one another, *Dao mohe difang qu?* Where are you going? And the response would be, *Dao Mohe difang qu,* I'm going Somewhere, or, *Dui, Mohe difang,* That's right: I'm going Somewhere ... In Mohe this was considered a good laugh.

Xue reflected that he and his men and on the other side Piotr (he couldn't remember the Russian's last name) and his had faced each other when the two countries were empires, they had faced each other when the two were 'fraternal socialist regimes', again as 'spittist' (Soviets on the Chinese) and 'revisionist' (Chinese on the Soviets) regimes, and the hapless guards were still here now as both countries peered ahead to uncertain futures; the Soviet Union having disintegrated into its constituent polities, and the People's Republic withdrawing into sullen isolation following the crushing of the Tian An Men demonstrations in 1989. No doubt when the Chinese embraced some form of capitalism – illicit thought! – Xue and his counterparts would still be standing here facing each other. Or rather someone would be standing here; Xue would be long gone. He hoped he would be an engineer or running a small business by then.

Xue was from Sichuan, a province that also had its wild areas, but nothing had prepared him for the steppes of Heilongjiang. He and private Hu were standing on the iron bridge. The water flowing beneath was grey-brown. Across the river an ash-coloured expanse stretched to the horizon. It was snowing lightly. If he had had the energy to look over his shoulder he would have seen the same plains and foothills extending to the south punctuated by the occasional grove of evergreens, the same lightly-falling snow. No matter which way one looked there was a desultory sameness to the region.

And the cold. It was wearing them all down, Chinese and Russians alike. Perhaps this was because on both the Chinese and Russian sides most of the border guards were not from this area. Most of the Russians were from west of the Ural mountains, the Chinese from south of the Great Wall. Their bodies were cold, their clothes froze, their minds definitely froze, and even the women they slept with (although of course there was no prostitution in either of the fraternal regimes) were frozen.

With nothing to fear and noses blue and minds lethargic and clothes stiff and local women icy, all the more reason to maintain a sense of humour, and both contingents clung to this lifeline. There was some communication between the two companies, consulations several times per week regarding cross-border traffic, visa formalities, bandit or fugitive activity. Each side had one or two of the men who spoke the other's language. Xue wasn't about to study Russian just for the sake of this four-year tour in the nether regions, but he had four-eyed Liu Xiting to translate, and the other side had some portly blond-haired fellow who spoke atrocious, toneless Chinese but who was coherent, and an enlisted man who was a Buriat Mongol who did somewhat better.

The two units would trade jibes, some of them a little too close to the truth to be entirely comfortable, but it was all nothing more than a way to relieve boredom. The shouts of the translators would gust back and forth across the bridge:

'Sure, this year, anyway . . . And what's new over there, Genghis?'

The first time he had heard this Xue's Manchurian cap had almost blasted off the top of his head in indignation. How dare this barbarian associate Xue with some Mongols (even though the Mongols had until recently been fraternal socialist brothers) trotting about the steppes munching on raw horsemeat! He was a Han Chinese, whose ancestors had written poetry on paper and used printing presses when Piotr's tribe was still beating off tigers with sticks.

'Nothing. Everything's fine. We got a new movie in.' A brand new film on the life of former premier Zhou Enlai.

'How is Deng, still playing bridge down in Peking?'

China's leading behind-the-scenes elder statesman was known to be an avid bridge player. 'Sure.' Since Xue had had the thought about the tiger, a recent incident came to mind: 'My men thought they saw a tiger last week.'

Coming back to Mohe in the open-backed truck, Xue had for a change been sitting back with four of the men when the vehicle hit the brakes abruptly. All five in the rear piled up together, a sprawl of arms and legs and jiggling Manchurian caps, a wriggling ten-limbed monster. What the hell!

wondered Xue. Then they heard the driver shouting something like *HU!* Then, *'Laohu!'* Tiger! Someone's cigarette had fallen out of their mouth and was rolling across the floor; corporal Feng was looking about sheepishly.

'Pick up the cigarette,' pointed Captain Xue; keep the men orderly even in a crisis!

The men had untangled themselves and four heads now protruded this way and that from the rear of the truck as Xue jumped down and went to the cab. He caught sight of an animal – probably a wolf, he thought – running through the firs to the north. 'Tiger!' repeated the driver.

'Yes, you said that.' Xue banged on the passenger-side door and the second soldier opened the door and moved over to make room as the officer climbed in out of the snow.

'Have you gone crazy, Bai?' Xue gave the driver no time to reply. 'There hasn't been a tiger here in over forty years!' To the second man: 'What do you say?'

'I didn't see clearly through the snow, but something ran across the road. We didn't want to hit it—'

'Renmin Jiefang Jun . . .' The People's Liberation Army, muttered Xue. He made a sardonic pun: *'Zheige bu shi Renmin Jiefang Jun, shi Renmin Jiefang zhou!'* This isn't the People's Liberation Army, these are the People's Liberation clowns!

'It looked like a tiger . . .' persisted the driver, eyes downcast.

'All right, Bai. Let's go. No one was hurt.' And the most important point: 'Dinner's waiting.'

At the gate of the border guards' small camp the sentry in the long overcoat shouted *Shei?'* Who is it? in accordance with the regulations but was left speechless when Xue leaned out the cab window and responded, 'The People's Liberation clowns.'

'We haven't seen any tigers lately,' came the voice of the Russian translator from the north bank of the Black Dragon River, 'except for the new commanding officer. He's a man who diligently follows procedure, a rousing example to his charges . . .'

'We have those tigers too,' commiserated Xue via the bespectacled corporal Liu

And so forth.

It was not that nothing ever happened at the Mohe bridge. These days with increasing frequency the Russians would let someone cross into China to do a little trading. These few inevitably returned to Siberia. Then, rarely, there was the odd case of someone or other being permitted to leave Russia via their humble border post. This occurred only ocasionally. What became of these poor wretches Heaven only knew. Xue had escorted one of them back to Mohe, again in the truck.

He had been a wizened old man huddled on the bench with a small valise at his feet. 'Where are we going?' he asked.

'Tell him we're going "Somewhere",' Xue blandly ordered corporal Liu.

Liu repeated this in Russian

'You mean you won't tell me—?'

It was very difficult to explain the joke . . .

Then, in the collection of thirty wooden buildings that was Mohe, the refugee was seated before Major Lang, the Ministry of State Security officer, a forbidding individual, and the old man's face fell when he saw him: he knew without any introductions who Major Lang was. He had met many Langs in his own land.

Rapallo

C. K. STEAD

Discussing Ezra

In the Rapallo post office a day or two before the opening of the 15th International Ezra Pound Conference I got into conversation with a local, there to collect his pension. He had known Pound – used to walk up the salita with him to Sant' Ambrogio. 'He was a very nice man – very charming.' I said his daughter, Mary de Rachewiltz, would be at the conference. He said he thought Pound had lived at Sant' Ambrogio 'with someone who was not his daughter'. 'No,' I agreed. 'She was his daughter's mother.' 'Ah yes. Well, he was a very nice man.'

A marble plaque over the passage from the Rapallo seafront to the Via Marsala records the many years Pound lived there. If you walk along the promenade, as Pound did every week before the war, and up the steep salita, up through terraced olive groves to the Church of Sant' Ambrogio sitting high over the town, you find, along the road to San Pantaleo, another plaque celebrating

Pound's occupancy. There is some overlap of dates. On the whole Pound lived in the seafront apartment with his wife Dorothy, and visited his friend (mistress, she would at that time have been called) violinist Olga Rudge at Sant' Ambrogio. But the exigencies of war were to push the three unhappily together; and even for a time a fourth, Mary, daughter to Pound and Olga, who during her infancy and childhood had been fostered by a peasant family in the Austrian/Italian Tirol.

Also down in the town, on the Corso Colombo, can be found a plaque recording that Yeats spent some part of each year there from 1928 to 1930. It quotes his tribute to Rapallo's beauty, and his question 'In what better place could I spend what winters yet remain?'. The Yeats-Pound connection was through Olivia Shakespear, the married woman who had relieved Yeats of the virginity, or anyway the chastity, which his love for Maud Gonne had seemed to require. Around 1912–13 Pound acted as Yeats's unpaid secretary; and Dorothy, whom Pound married, was Olivia's daughter.

There is nothing on the Corso Colombo to show that Pound's parents also lived there for a time after the father, Homer Pound, retired; but in the *reparto acattolico* of the town cemetery Homer's grave is to be found, the ivy which covered the headstone (surmounted by what appears to be a death mask) pulled back by those of us arriving at the conference early enough to have made prior visits to significant sites. The gravestone makes no mention of Ezra. It records that Homer was born in Chippewa Falls, 26.8.1858, died Rapallo 25.2.1942, and that his wife, Isabel Weston Pound, now resided at Gais in the Tirol. That was because by the time the stone. was ordered the war was over, Pound was in Washington awaiting trial for treason, or possibly already locked up in St Elizabeth's Hospital for the Insane; and Isabel who until necessity required it had never acknowledged nor looked upon her son's daughter-out-of-wedlock, was now living with her in the mountains. According to the daughter's book,* Isabel was carried the last stage of her journey to Gais on a 'sedan-like contraption' made 'by passing the long poles of rakes and pitchforks between the slats of a deck-chair' – 'stately, erect, like the Empress Dowager, followed by more men carrying trunks.' Isabel spent her last days reading and re-reading *Don Quixote,* instructing her grand-daughter how to poach an egg, and planning a canal from Venice to Milan 'big enough for big boats to navigate with their cargo'. Clearly she was the mother of the *Cantos*.

Pound's dilemma when America entered the War is characterized by that web of personal connections he had created around himself since moving to Rapallo in 1923 – a wife, a mistress, two aged parents (and he their only child). A firm supporter of Mussolini, he was making regular broadcasts over Rome Radio, in his bizarre way attempting to prevent his own country from entering the conflict. He might at that point have elected Italian citizenship, which would have removed the possibility of a treason charge later on; but he believed himself a loyal American, serving America's interests. He might have made a last-

*Discretions, Mary de Rachewiltz. Faber. 1971.

minute return to the United States; but his old father had broken a hip and could not be moved; and how would the wife/mistress arrangement have been dealt with? He might have accepted that silence was now required of him; but he had persuaded himself that by continuing to broadcast he was upholding an American's right to free speech. And in any case the widening gap between the world as it was and as he wanted it to be was causing him increasing confusion, driving him to frenzy.

There is a pause in the broadcasts, and then they are resumed – uglier, more impassioned, full of Douglas Social Credit and anti-Semitism (usury was the source of all the world's ills, including the war, and the creation of credit the solution); but so confused, random and paranoid that some officials in Rome questioned whether this loyal ally of Fascist Italy might in truth be a secret agent sending messages in code.

Opening the conference in the beautiful municipal Salone where Pound organised concerts (Olga played, Dorothy was patron) Professor Massimo Bacigalupo of the University of Genoa spoke of Rapallo's place in the poetry. He described finding, in Yale, a cancelled passage in the MSS of one of the Cantos recounting how, at the time when Italy first surrendered to the Allies, Pound had borrowed from one Massimo Bacigalupo, the local chemist and the professor's grandfather, a copy he owned of the Rapallo newspaper of 1815 recording the return of Napoleon from Elba. The point was that Pound hoped for a similar return of his hero. And he got his wish. The Germans rescued Mussolini and set him up in the north as head of the Salo republic – 'thus' (Bacigalupo remarked) 'condemning Italy to two years of civil war'.

It was at this time that Pound walked, rode the rail-cars, hitch-hiked, sleeping rough, from Rome, where he had been broadcasting, up into the Tirol to tell his daughter the truth thus far concealed from her about her intermittent parents – that they were not married, that there was a wife. Then he headed for Mussolini's new centre of power. He was back in Rapallo some considerable time later when the Allied armies arrived. Partisans arrested him, and must have considered summary execution. As he was marched down the salita to be handed to the Americans he picked up a eucalypt seed from a tree still to be seen there, thinking it might be all he would take of Italy back to America. It was buried with him in Venice almost thirty years later.

From Rapallo the sixty-year-old poet was taken to the US Army Detention centre at Pisa and locked in the famous wire cage. After a period that brought him close to breakdown he was given more space, and the use of the dispensary typewriter at night, on which he composed, or typed up from handwritten drafts, the *Pisan Cantos*. This was during the months that passed before he was flown to Washington to face the capital charge of treason, from which he escaped only by the decision to pronounce him insane.

Hugh Kenner's contribution to the conference opening, apart from the picturesque flurry of a late arrival, was to offer 'a fact and a piece of wisdom'. The fact, which I suppose most Poundians know, was the one about the eucalypt seed. The piece of wisdom was something Pound had written to him many years ago: that ninety per cent of those things we perceive as requiring to be done can be achieved within twenty-four hours of the recognition of the need. It was, Kenner said, a corrective against saying 'I haven't found the time.' I found myself wondering what it was Pound had wanted to bully the young Kenner into doing at the time it was offered.

Kenner might have stopped there, but he went on. He said he had no idea why an Australian tree should be growing in Rapallo (in fact eucalypts were planted along that coast, once a resort for tuberculosis sufferers, because they were thought to purify the air); but he offered an explanation why Pound used it as a symbol of memory. 'Eucalypt' meant 'well-covered', 'concealed', 'enclosed'. Memory was something enclosed in the mind. And there was some further etymological connection made with Calypso – Pound as Odysseus, Calypso the nymph who detained him. It was a typical Kenner exercise, appealing to the intellect, but conducted at the outer perimeter of plausibility, where common sense declines to dance. What, after all, were the circumstances? Pound, under arrest, his life in danger, picks up the seed thinking he will have, at least, a memento, one whose strong scent will go on evoking that scene, its stone walls and olive groves, its brilliant views down to the town of Rapallo and the cape running away past Santa Margherita to Portofino. The facts, simple in themselves, have the sort of complexity which only the human mind, collaborating with the senses in looking forward to looking back, is capable of. Is more needed? Or (as often happens in literary studies) are invented complexities blurring and spoiling the real ones?

I walked up there twice during the conference, thinking not only of Pound trudging up and back, his life lived 'between a door and a door', but of the image Mary de Rachewiltz offers of the courageous and persistent Olga Rudge (who is alive aged ninety-eight) tucking up her formal dress after a concert in the town, changing out of her best shoes, strapping her violin case to her back and tramping up to the house at Sant' Ambrogio. On those hill paths life has become mythology quite as much as it has along the coast at Lerici where Shelley's drowned corpse was burned on the beach and Byron plucked the heart from it to be kept by the grieving widow.

On the second day of the conference Professor Bacigalupo invited me, with Mary de Rachewiltz, to his house up in the hills where his wife and a friend were preparing lunch. Once there we could see the church of Sant' Ambrogio away to the east and at a lower level. In the garden, where the table was set under a rattan screen, I told Mary de Rachewiltz that on the flight from Auckland to Rome I had re-read her book, and how much I admired its crisp style and the way it was put together. She said, with a Poundian forthrightness and succinctness, that unfortunately most Pound scholars saw it as a resource, not as a piece of writing.

She told me she had received an advance for it and had used the money to fly to Africa leaving all papers and source material behind so that it would be

written from memory and thus unified – all but the part she called the 'war diary', which belonged to its time. This accorded with my own thoughts about the *Pisan Cantos*: that the great sense of a unity, a perfect focus in them, which so many of the earlier Cantos lack, is explained not only by the shock of Pound's incarceration and the sense of loss which the end of the Fascist 'dream' meant to him, but even more by the circumstances of the Detention Centre, which deprived him of reference books. The *Pisan Cantos* are an extraordinary feat of memory. But memory is not just the reservoir; it is also the filter.

It is a view not always welcomed by Poundians becasuse it implies a negative corollary: that large sections of the earlier *Cantos* lack shape and focus, wrecked by a linear accretion of material as Pound returned again and again to his book-sources while engaged in the writing.

They were good people at the 15th Conference – good talkers, good listeners, good carousers; and there was very little of the theoretical language which entangles and impedes so much current academic discussion of poems and fictions. Pound liked exposition to be concrete, particular, emphatic, and perhaps his devotees learn from his example.

But there is a defensiveness and protectiveness among those who study and write about Pound. Hugh Kenner is the most brilliant; he has made wonderful narrative of the history of anglophone Modernism, placing Pound, justly, at the centre. But for him Pound can do no wrong; every word is holy writ. This refusal to recognise limit springs partly, I suppose, from the knowledge of how strong, and often ignorant, prejudice against Pound has been, and remains. But my own view is that prejudice is best defused by freely acknowledging the unsatisfactory elements of Pound which promote it. Then it becomes possible to argue plausibly for the much that remains which is good, original, valuable, rewarding – and sometimes beautiful, with the beauty of the very greatest poetry.

For Pound, all experience came back to language, and language was unstable. It came in through the ear, in different accents and with different emphases, and every word or phrase carried with it the shadow of other sounds, other meanings, a different history, another language. So verbal structures were like social structures – a set of conventions, a pretence at permanence and stability which might at any moment break down. They were buildings that creaked and swayed when the wind blew. The pun, the double-entendre, word-play, verbal shiftiness, represented the universal comedy of our insecure hold on order. And I think this was a recognition much more available to an American of the early twentieth century than to a European. Pound's assertive 'Amurkinism', which caused lips to curl and eyebrows to be raised, had an intellectual base. A man could walk on water; but only so long as confidence – which meant health, vital energy, testosterone – lasted. Pound lived on after those vital juices and energies had run out. Those were the last sad years, the years of his long silences, out of which he emerged only rarely,

usually to say that his life had been a waste and a failure.

Pound's philosophical base was scepticism; its principle was uncertainty, indeterminacy; and his talent was correspondingly lyrical, not epic. His great error was to propose solutions to the world's ills, and to attempt to project them on an epic scale. In that he betrayed his own genius; but that did not prevent him from writing some of the century's greatest poetry.

Theatre

ANTHONY CURTIS

David Hare

At the age of twenty-one when he came down from Cambridge in 1968 David Hare co-founded Portable Theatre, a group that travelled around the country putting on plays in a basic style with a minimum of scenery. He became literary manager of the Royal Court Theatre in 1969 and its resident dramatist in 1970. Among his colleagues were William Gaskill, Max Stafford-Clark, David Aukin, and the four founded the Joint Stock Theatre Group – 'for what purpose', says Gaskill in *Sense of Direction* (1988) 'no one was quite sure but Max kept calling it "an umbrella organisation".'

Joint Stock's first production, *The Speakers,* was a play in which most of the dialogue was drawn from a book of that name by Heathcote Williams containing transcripts of Sunday orators in Hyde Park. The success of that venture encouraged Hare to make a play out of William Hinton's study of the inhabitants of the Chinese village of Long Bow during the Revolution. The outcome was *Fanshen* first performed in London by Joint Stock directed by Gaskill and Stafford-Clark in 1975 at the ICA. Gaskill explained the process through which the book was made into the scripted play:

[It was] . . . a method which became known as the Joint Stock Process: a workshop in which the material was explored, researched and improvised around, a gap in which the writer went away and wrote the play, and an extended rehearsal period of a more conventional kind. From the beginning David had a very firm sense of the structure of the book and perhaps of the eventual play.

'I tried in *Fanshen*' says Hare 'to write a classical play about revolution, setting out the problems which will always arise when people try to change the relationship between leadership and the led.' As such it was successful in spite of a huge list of changes to the text demanded by Hinton when he saw the play performed in Sheffield. He wanted it to have more marxist and less liberal flavour. What was notable from the technical angle was the simplicity of the method used to dramatise the politically sensitive material – no sets, no lighting cues, nine actors playing thirty parts. An entire society could be represented on stage in this economical way. Michael Coveney writing about it in *Plays and Players* felt that it was 'the nearest an English contemporary writer has come to emulating Brecht'. In anglicizing the Brechtian method of dramatic representation Hare had done a marvellous thing; somehow he had eliminated the boredom that so often

accompanies it. In the hands of the Berliner Ensemble Brecht is not boring, far from it, but in lesser hands in translation he easily becomes so.

Hare's mature plays are all exposures of the various dishonesties, betrayals, rackets, confidence tricks inherent in contemporary society, but his active social conscience has never prevented him experimenting with form, drawing on a variety of models for his stagecraft. Hare chastens his audiences but he is concerned that they should enjoy themselves. He never loses sight of the fun, the ludic element essential to successful play-writing. A sense of an up-graded Noël Coward entertainment could be found in Hare's first hit *Slag* (1971), an almost plotless three-hander, containing a rapid fire of one-liners concerning women's rights and revolutionary feminism, delivered by a trio of schoolmistresses. In *Teeth'n'Smiles* (1975), one of several forays into the drug culture, there was an alliance with Rock. The musicians were members of the cast with speaking roles; their music and lyrics were contributed by Nick and Tony Bicât. In *The Great Exhibition* (1972) the framework was from Black Mask, the old private eye pulp fiction magazine but transposed to post-war Clapham. The hero was called Hammett; he was an ex-Labour MP, and a compulsive flasher. The same hard-boiled manner appeared to good effect in *Knuckle* where the setting was the seedier side of Eastbourne.

As Hare's confidence has grown so has the gulf between the model and the message. Only Hare, surely, would have had the nerve to structure a play whose ostensible subject is the Third World debt crisis on Pirandello's planes of reality, as he did in *A Map of the World* (1982). Each delegate at an international conference in Bombay on the debt problem also plays the part of an actor playing the role in a feature film that is being made from a book based on the conference. Economics mixed with pirandellist histrionics proved to be an oddly flavoured cocktail that some members of the audience found hard to swallow.

Hare's lens as a playwright is sharply focused but wide-angle; he regards the whole contemporary Global Village as potential material. He must be the least insular playwright we have ever had, even though he has often found material in aspects of recent British history. Looking back to the second world war (he was not born until after it was over) in *Licking Hitler,* he has revealed the corrosion of personal probity suffered by those who operated the black propaganda broadcasting unit, while in *Plenty* he explored the difficulty for a woman of leading a 'normal' post-war domestic life after once having worked on parachute-drops in SOE. The attitudes of Thatcherite Britain were conflated with the fate of a country house in *Secret Rapture.*

In 1986, slightly against Hare's will, his publishers, grouped *Fanshen, A Map of the World* and *Saigon: Year of the Cat* – three works that had quite separate origins – in a single volume they called *The Asian Plays. Saigon,* a film shown on Thames Television in 1983, dramatised the chain of events through which the Americans finally pulled out of Vietnam; the impact of the withdrawal on a group of British and American people working

there, some of whom got left behind in the final scramble. Hare spent much time in Vietnam researching this piece. Most of these works showed how conscientiously Hare applies the techniques of the investigative journalist to the task of play-writing, and this is particularly true of *The David Hare Trilogy* first performed in its entirety at the Royal National Theatre in October 1993. The three plays, *Racing Demon, Murmuring Judges* and *The Absence of War,* originally performed separately, are concerned with the workings of three great British institutions, the Church, the Law and the State; or more specifically, an inner London team ministry, the criminal justice system, and a general election.

This ambitious trilogy grew out of a development of the Joint Stock method long after the end of Hare's period with Joint Stock. His standing as a playwright gained him the *entrée* into such strictly no-go areas to outsiders as the policy meetings of the Parliamentary Labour Party and the charge room of Clapham Police Station. Either naivety or vanity seems to have prevented the authorities from seeing how damaging the presence of Hare, a very accurate observer of what is happening around him, could be to the public image of the places he attended. He ended with far more material than he could use in the plays and has published it as a book, *Asking Around: Background to the David Hare Trilogy* (Faber £8.99). Whether one has seen the plays or not the book is an Orwellian eye-opener. There are transcripts of days Hare spent at the General Synod, the Church of England's equivalent of Parliament, where the standard of debate is higher, the jokes subtler and the atmosphere less rowdy than the House of Commons; and there are records of long nights talking to cops who were busy planning their skiing holidays while rounding up the drunks and the junkies. There is a detailed description of a dinner at High Table at Middle Temple, one of the Inns of Court where Hare was a guest. ('They seem to do themselves very well there'.)

What is interesting is the separation between this raw material and the finished plays where the play-writer's imagination has been hard at work ditching much of what the journalist has discovered or developing merely one aspect of it. Hare initiated his investigation of the Church of England by looking into the suicide of Gareth Bennett, the author of the anonymous preface to *Crockford's* critical of the church's liberal hierarchy. He ended with something much more topical and promising dramatically, the system of team ministries whereby clergy whose parishes are in inner city areas work together pooling their skills and resources like group practices in the National Health Service. In direct contact with much heart-rending human misery the clergymen involved easily become less concerned with worship and doctrine than with counselling and providing practical help to members of their flock who are in distress.

Hare's Rev Lionel Espy, played by the tall, bald, gangling Oliver Ford Davies, a brilliant character-actor, becomes so absorbed in this pastoral, social worker side of his job that it begins to undermine his faith, and his command in church of his congregation as a whole, and he thereby gets into very hot water with his bishop (suavely executed by Richard Pasco).

Hare's research into conditions of work led him to uncover an interesting legal point about the team ministries. Their existence affects the principle by which a clergyman appointed to a parish gets the freehold of it. In normal circumstances he cannot ever be removed, but for team ministries tenure becomes renewable at the discretion of the bishop. In ninety-nine cases out of a hundred this renewal is a formality. In *Racing Demon* Hare posits the hundredth case. The play is powered by the spectacle of a time-bomb ticking away under Lionel that will blow him right out of his job in the most humiliating circumstances. He gains the sympathy of the audience from the moment he enters and addresses not them but God:

God. Where are you? I wish you would talk to me. God. It isn't just me. There's a general feeling. This is what people are saying in the parish. They want to know where you are. The joke wears thin.

This trick of allowing each of the principal characters — including the other three members of the Team, who are a homosexual priest (Michael Bryant), an old-style Anglican padre (Adrian Scarborough) and a young modern Christian fundamentalist (Adam Kotz) — to pray aloud is a typical Hare *trouvaille* exclusive to this play. Through characters audibly engaged in prayer Hare revives the soliloquy, and penetrates the recesses of his people's minds without self-consciousness. We are conditioned to accept such moments before the play begins in Richard Eyre's excellent production. As we enter the auditorium we observe that it resembles the nave of a church; the seats are arranged in a cruciform shape. This was particularly effective at the adaptable Cottesloe Theatre auditorium where the play originally opened in February 1990 and from which the Trilogy evolved.

The validity of its translation to the larger Olivier Theatre lies in the power of *Racing Demon* and the two other plays to hold and move audiences, to provoke a national debate outside of the theatre, to arouse hostile comment from those whose entrenched professional positions the plays expose. No question here of the Right to Fail. The whole *Trilogy* is a roaring success attracting capacity business. All three plays are stimulating contemporary drama full of good performances but *Racing Demon* does have a depth lacking in *Murmuring Judges* and *The Absence of War*. The latter seem, for much of the time, to be more like tv documentaries that have somehow found their way onto the stage; whereas in *Demon* we really are moved to tears, and not just by Lionel's plight but by those of his colleagues as well, even by the novice whose naive new broom-like enthusiasm for the job precipitates Lionel's downfall. The scene at the Savoy Grill where the two oldies try to nobble this Judas over sunrise cocktails has a satirical edge as sharp as anything Hare has ever written.

In all three plays it is the men's roles that hog the action but this is not so much a criticism of Hare as of the institutions he is putting on stage. His earlier plays showed he is capable of writing very demanding parts for women. In *Racing Demon* the two supporting female roles, that of Lionel's wife Heather and Frances, the girlfriend of the young zealot, gave great opportunities to Barbara Leigh-Hunt and Saskia Wickham. The domestic lives of those within the church were illuminated with an authority unseen in the theatre since *Candida*.

In *Murmuring Judges* a police-woman (Kastrina Levon) and a black trainee barrister (Alphonsia Emmanuel) enabled Hare to introduce a note of female compassion into what is basically a Ludovic Kennedy-type account of yet one more miscarriage of British justice concerning an IRA suspect. The alleged crime and its consequences are followed through at all levels – the Old Bailey, the police station, the defending barrister's chambers, the reception area of the prison, its cells and shower blocks. Bob Crowley, the designer, and Mark Douet, responsible for projections, are given their heads and do a fine job; the cuts and switchings from one environment to another are smoothly cinematic. Once again it is a festive scene – all at a legal reception – that provides the keenest irony.

At the start of *Absence of War* the audience is prepared for what is to follow by a full-scale simulation of the ceremony at the Cenotaph on Remembrance Sunday when the Sovereign and the leaders of all three political parties line up together and lay their wreaths at the foot of the memorial. It is a solemn framing moment of harmony and silence for a piece that plunges us into the political maelstrom at its most frenetic, the period just before and during the three weeks' campaign at a General Election. When Hare started his research he aimed to cover all the main political parties but once admitted to the secret conclaves of the Labour Party after the election had been called he realised he would have to stay with them, and observe the others from the outside.

Hare developed great admiration for Neil Kinnock. In the play he gives us in the fictitious labour leader George Jones – a memorable performance by John Thaw – someone who both is and is not Kinnock. The problem, as Hare conceives it, for the real man and the imaginary one, was to stop themselves from becoming trapped by the strategists and the image-makers. At the beginning of the play a professional imagist in the shape of Clare Higgins is engaged to give the party a face-lift. As her influence grows, the way the leader is manipulated by her and his senior colleagues, some loyal and some not (Oliver Ford Davies re-appears here as one of them) gives Hare the bones of his narrative. He creates the mounting campaign fever, the utter dependence of everyone concerned on the current findings of the opinion polls, most authentically, but that has been done before by playwrights like Dennis Potter and David Edgar. It is in his portrait of the leader that Hare is at his most original. It is not perhaps surprising that Hare, consummate man of the theatre, should show how inextricably success in politics is linked to the art of performance, and that the mainspring of performance must be conviction.

Art

IAN JEFFREY

Sincerity

Larry Clark's *The Perfect Childhood* * asks for your full attention. But is it art, or is it outrage? It is a book of 178 (unpaginated) pages, hosting a 31-page narration, in monochrome, of a US teen blow job: long-haired girl-next-door on a slender proto-surfer in a beaded necklace. You might imagine prurience, but it is more of a documentary, artlessly shot. Its virtue is its naiveté. Anyone engrossed by American culture must be sick, by now, of its preoccupations with inauthenticity, smothered in brand-names (Bret Easton Ellis) or dissolved in talk (Don Delillo).

This is not to claim that *The Perfect Childhood* is the real thing, through and through. A lot of its colour pages are of such teen stars as Matt Dillon and the late River Phoenix, and Clark is attentive to the difference between Hollywood's ideas of adolescence and his own experience. There is nothing censorious about his approach. He, too, seems to see the tanned Hollywood adolescent as some kind of an ideal. All he does, it appears, is to situate that ideal among his versions of the actualities of growing up in California and Oklahoma. He doesn't insist on the bland adolescent idol as a phantasm to be denounced even though he does give the other side of the story in a set of collages along

*LCB, 80 Charing Cross Road, WC2. £35.00.

such lines as 'Texas teen's sadistic murder'. In fact, his attitude is hard to establish, for page after page recounts little more than normative teenage male faces and scabbed knees. Perhaps he is just being as good as his word and sketching in an idea of a perfect childhood in which you also get to kill your parents.

No – that is to invest him with too much of an attitude. He does include his collages of adolescent outrages, but they are included rather than related. They take their places with everything else in a comprehensive assemblage which pays equal attention to the ideal and the actual. You can't come away from the experience heartened or even informed. For a start there is a lot of Clark himself in the survey including his data from the Smither's Centre in which he admits to the use of twenty-eight different kinds of drugs from mid-youth onwards – ending with an excess of crack in 1990. The records also say that he was given five years in the McAlester Penitentiary in 1977 (reduced to nineteen months) for violence, drugs and sexual excess. The drugs list is interesting on a lot of grounds, but it does make you wonder that someone recollecting in 1990 can recall taking a shot of numarophine five times in 1971, and sylsibin three times in 1968–69. In the book McAlester Pen. comes up in the shape of three letters from a former cell-mate, Larry Miller, writing about 'the Church of Nature, which I am going to form'.

What is he up to? In one collage two teenage torsoes with erections back a letter from Peter MacGill of the Pace/MacGill Gallery: 'Few people are able to combine appropriated imagery with their own work and make a clear statement with it. I like the challenge of this new work and look forward to seeing more in the future.' You can imagine a gallerist taking a guarded attitude to the new work of September 1989. Clark might have enjoyed the clichés, but he's no satirist, and most of the texts are miniaturised enough to make reading difficult.

The absorbing thing about *The Perfect Childhood* is that it is sincere. Clark's childhood experiences are of real interest to him. He suffered, and he would like you to know. Another collage contains a notional letter written to his absent father. Clark was, it seems, a late developer who worried his parents: 'Why did I wake up one night in bed with Mary Lou looking up my asshole with a flashlight? Looking for worms or parasites that only comes out when you're asleep?' The big problem, apparently, involved pubic hair: 'All I know was why didn't I grow up and have hair on my dick like my chums.'

The Perfect Childhood is garrulous, scabrous and demotic, packed with reference to teen-culture, drug-culture and the hero's personal mishaps. It's as if the author wanted to engage at all costs, and had hit on lurid personal recollections as the way through. His audience, under these terms, is someone who wants the whole truth, and wants it now – hence the therapeutic notes on that troubled childhood, and that drug laden data base. Adolescence, that is to say, might be his ostensible topic, but *horror vacui* is his subject. Clark constitutes, in *The Perfect Childhood,* a one-man Biennale of distractions. He is, in this respect, the real thing, the founding artist of this moment; and it is no surprise that he was interviewed by Mike Kelley at some length – apparently for this book. In the Kelley interview – shown me by a Zwemmers' agent – the younger artist (described recently in the *New Yorker* as the most imitated of all established artists) is respectful of the old hand, even cowed. Clark, for his part, acts like an avatar of Lenny Bruce, though without the climaxes: 'I remember when I got it – I was about 37 years old. And all of a sudden I realized I was mortal, I could die, and I cared. I got sick, I got very sick, and I realized . . . Well, my body broke down, I couldn't believe it. I was 37 years old and my body broke down, I had ulcers and pancreatitis, and I almost died from it. And my whole thing was cast iron stomach, I can drink all I want to, I can do anything I want to, nothing can kill me, nothing can hurt me. And I was like one of those guys that was able to do that with no problems at all, until I was 37, and one day, bang, boy, it hit me, and I realized that all my friends, and all people that I knew, who hadn't died earlier, if they kept like shooting dope or doing heroin, died about 37 or 38. Nobody got past that point. That was like a limit. And I'm saying, gee, everybody died earlier, the toughest guys died early, then a couple of them made it to 37, 38, but there's a cut-off point, and I made it that far, so I guess I'm gonna die right now.'

If you want to trace the present moment to its roots – and there is a lot of ferreting and blaming going on just now – you need look no further than Larry Clark. *Tulsa* (1971) was his first book, on the drug scene in that city, and *Teenage Lust* (1983) his most recent – on that topic. Not that Clark is greatly heard of, for *Tulsa* was a low-run independent publication, and he is a photographer, which is to say a self-elected marginal. But it was Clark who gave accreditation to the sordid extremism of grunge. He lived an art, where others only acted, and opted for reality at a time when artifice was in: 'Oh, too real', was the response from the Warhol Factory. It is only because of an artist like Clark that young contemporaries can act bad. Somewhere, they know, there's a sanctioned backing for their currency. Duchamp of the Ivory Towers is most often quoted, but Tulsa and McAlester Pen. have far better claims to that responsibility.

*   *   *

One of the big puzzles of the 1990s is political art, and there was a chance to reflect on it in *Wall to Wall,* a show of wall drawings and site specific works at the Serpentine Gallery (19 January–27 February). *Wall to Wall* hosted two prime political artists: the German Lothar Baumgarten and the American Barbara Kruger. The temptation is simply to put the boot in and then hope for a job with the *Evening Standard.* On the other hand there might be something to be said on their behalf, as for their colleagues: Michael Craig-Martin, Jessica Diamond, Niele Tooini and Lawrence Weiner. My suspicion, at least, is that the politicals are not what they seem. At first sight they seem like simpletons.

Baumgarten is well known internationally, and ought to be of concern here since the Tate acquired a large (and expensive) piece by him two years ago – on the exploitation of rain forests in Brazil. I was told that the Serpentine room is his first ever site specific work in this country, and thus noteworthy. But to any regular broadsheet reader his installation, entitled *Imago Mundi* and given in sparse, bold lettering on walls and ceiling of the Serpentine rotunda can only have looked (A) unfathomable and then (B) platitudinous. His topic was colonialism, due to London having recently been the capital of a great empire.

Overhead were printed L'AUTRE ET L'AILLEURS. Then above the cornice were the names of countries, including France, England and Holland, and below were the names of continents – everywhere but Europe. There was what appeared to be an acknowledgement of the Kodak Company of Rochester, NY, and in the clerestory windows some coloured panes of glass had been fitted. Make something of this, *Imago Mundi* commanded. Of course, there wasn't much hope of making anything of it until you went to the brochure, which gave it to you in no uncertain terms. The countries, by the rubric, were colonizers and the continents colonized. The bits of coloured glass related to the names of printers' basic colours – cyan, yellow, magenta, black – stencilled on the walls. The brochure held that the colours 'stand for the colours of the peoples of the earth and the countries and continents they inhabit'. The printing tie-up was with Kodak and the implication was that tourism (signalled by photography) is a suc-

cessor to colonialism. Elliptical and vertiginous.

Hang on Lothar. People may believe these things, and even take them for granted, but is it wise to replicate them thus? Baumgarten's reply might be (I hope) that you weren't paying attention, and that there were grey areas. For instance, America had climbed the cornice and joined the colonizing countries, whilst Spain and Portugal had sunk, and Portugal had even turned turtle. There are, he might be demonstrating, difficulties with simple conceptual schemes of the sort we often depend on. And he might go on to add that you were right to wonder if 'colonized' Asia had always been free from indigenous despotisms. And so for the poor old Kodak Company being a standard-bearer for post-colonialism – a travesty. You might as well blame Mercedes for contemporary tyrannies on the grounds that a lot of dubious political leaders use its products. In short, Baumgarten's truisms are given so elliptically, or with such huge intervals between word and meaning that they will put *anyone* to work on the truth behind the terms.

With contemporary product, though, there is often no telling. That rather knowing reading of Baumgarten might be wrong, and he might be simply trying to give his readers the truth about colonialism, and then about its relation to tourism. That's what the brochure says, and presumably its writer had access to the artist's ideas. I don't believe it – I can't believe it. Look at it this way: *Imago Mundi* is – like so much else in today's vanguard – a charade in which the artist has deployed a number of ideologically charged terms, such as L'AUTRE L'AILLEURS. Alerted, you fill in the background. You? Well, not exactly you, rather the exegetes who have done the work on your behalf. What you are being invited to participate in is an exchange between the artist and scholarship, in which you function as a spectator confronted by a mystery. The key to *Imago Mundi,* for instance, is the Guggenheim exhibition catalogue of early 1993, *America Invention,* in which Baumgarten's likely meanings are given in texts gravid with footnotes.

A game is being played in front of your eyes, and you might – if you could only get hold of the rule book – join in. The rule book, though, is written by Deleuze & Guattari, Lacan, Lyotard, etc., mediated by another range of tenured professors. Thus the likelihood is that you're going to remain a spectator. This impasse might explain the apparent naiveté of the other political. Barbara Kruger. She works with a rush of text, sans serif and in red, white and black, as if an imitation of more urgent days, *c.*1930. Her texts, lettered onto beams, walls and floors read like outbursts: 'Who knows that doubt tempers belief with sanity?' or 'Think Like Us. Look for the moment when pride becomes contempt.' She seems, that is, to have borrowed a totalitarian visual rhetoric and to have applied it to homilies, aphorisms, and terrible warnings. It's as if a warm-hearted evangelical had tried to go in disguise, as a sheep in wolf's clothing.

Kruger's virtue is uncertainty. The print style might be ancient totalitarian, but the homilies are at sixes and sevens. What exactly does she mean? Is what she says a warning, or is she warning against what she says? One minute she's giving forth like a demagogue, and the next you're shuffling around to read the prose beneath your feet.

What both her and Baumgarten appear to be doing – even if it's not given in any declared intention – is to relate thinking to acting and to moving. Kruger's floor, with its eight sentences, has virtually to be spelled out, and is hard to take at one go. Not only are you standing on the text, but others are too. And with Baumgarten there's just as much peering and craning and checking on sunlight filtered by the tinted glass. Jessica Diamond, more homiletic than political, makes similar demands, for her messages are written vertically and in circles, and in a cursive script difficult to make out. Lawrence Weiner, next door, seemed to deal in time, for his proposed proposal read A ROPE (OF HEMP) + A CABLE (OF STEEL) + A THREAD (OF SILK) & BRAIDED (ALL TOGETHER) block-capitaled into and onto the wall. There was no option but to read carefully for a moment or two, imagine briefly and move on. Michael Craig-Martin, cunning enough to be credited with the single-handed ruin of British art in recent years, then gave a synopsis of the show in the shape of a set of wall-drawings which told of reading as concentration and physical stasis. Radiator, chair, locker, filing cabinet, note-pad and book, all held within 'large fields of vibrant colour' (brochure), showed an idea of understanding (reading) suspended within the sensuous. Where the others were concerned to distinguish the message and its moments here, by contrast, reading and sensing were thoroughly mingled – or braided, Weiner might have said.

If *Wall to Wall* is about cognition, or about uncertainties before the written word, why does no one say so? The brochure, for example, took a positive, univocal view, and the catalogue seemed to set out to say next to nothing. Of course, to remark on uncertainty would dissolve the very uncertainty at issue. And uncertainty matters to artists, because their practice is under threat, less from reaction than from teams of exegetes out to make everything clear. Sooner or later they will catch hold of their prey, but in the meantime the victim can twist and turn – hence, perhaps, those folkish homilies from Kruger in their antipathetic context of dictatorial control, and hence too Baumgarten's provocative ellipses, blithe and bland against their background of theory. Ditto, art's relation to the culture at large broadcasting on all channels.

Wall to Wall's still point was a room of brushmarks in series and in echelon by Niele Toroni. Silence.

The show was organised by Maureen Paley, for the South Bank Centre, and sponsored – appropriately enough – by British Telecom, big in the message business. It is the first of three exhibitions under the same title: phase two goes on at the Southampton City Art Gallery, 22 April–1 June, and phase three at the Leeds City Art Gallery, 12 May–2 July.

*   *   *

Jimmie Durham is that rare thing, a Cherokee history artist. Funny, too – which is also rare amongst vanguardists. He exhibited at the ICA under the heading *Original Re-Runs.* After time in the navy, Durham worked as a furnace mechanic at the University of Texas, before moving to the École des Beaux-Arts in Geneva. Now a regular on the Documenta and Biennale circuit, he lives in Mexico (brochure details).

Art has been an oppressively serious business for a long time, probably because – and despite all the talk of 'international artists' – it has been increasingly hemmed into one part of the culture, which is the same everywhere, from Tokyo to the Beaubourg. Durham's advantage is that whilst he's a part of that world he is also familiar with, and seemingly rooted in, a quite different ethics.

He makes a peculiarly tangible art, out of bones, bits of found wood, glass eyes, scraps of wire and the like. Most of the pieces are small enough to handle, and in the pitiless lighting of the ICA looked out of place, like a Cherokee Surrealist house clearance brought into the lab for forensic tests.

The pieces are small and makeshift because they are meant as correctives to a dominant culture whose delusions come as generalities. The best way of standing out against these delusions is via particulars. Furthermore, particulars belong to the defeated culture, as he remarks: 'There is a mistaken idea that our traditional art is religious, that art objects are made for "magical purposes". Mostly our "gods" are real: animals, the sun and moon, the elements . . . What is called our "religion" is more practical and down-to-earth.'

The dominant culture is a behemoth, and poorly sighted, and it is going to keep going irrespective until Armageddon.

WE HAVE MADE
PROGRESS
AND WE WILL CONTINUE TO
PROGRESS

Durham's tactic is to oppose the brute with bits and pieces in parodies, for example, of level-headed protest. This was a text included in a display-case piece on Native American sociofacts: 'Traditionally, American Indians had many uses for water. It was used extensively in agriculture, for example. Many Indian tribes used water in various specialist dishes, such as soup or stew. It was also used for teas, cleaning and washing up. This is all changing now, of course, because the rivers that once went through Indian reservations are now being diverted to American cities and industrial complexes.'

It is a self-abnegating tactic, of de-liberate humility in the face of the Juggernaut, or the culture of cities and industrial complexes as opposed to that of soups and stews. He makes a show of himself as some kind of a primitive impressed by the organization, and in two or three pieces picks on the Pinkerton Agency as his target. Extracts from the Pinkerton code of practice are written out in a gauche, admiring hand and installed among shaky native-looking artefacts, as if they'd been found among the ruins. All the time Durham is having his revenge, and not simply through *faux naif* ironies. On the other hand he reports on vanishing cultures as a contemporary looking back, and then shifts his stance to present himself as a traveller in time returned decades hence to report on a desolated culture from which he can only salvage mysterious oddments and inscriptions: 'We have made progress and we will continue to progress' reads one of these salvaged placards. His tactic is to envisage the present as just another lost North American culture.

He dramatizes himself as an archaeologist exploring deep stretches pf past time to which the guides are imperfect and unconvincing. He seems to be at odds with Lothar Baumgarten, his more celebrated contemporary in the history business, to the extent of exhibiting a piece of crackly script in indigenous figures entitled 'Not Lother Baumgarten's Cherokee'. To the European, history is primarily something which can be understood as a system and *in toto*. One of Durham's main exhibits at the ICA was *Malinche*, a seated figure named after a Mexican Indian princess who, myth had it, had been Cortez's lover and translator. Built from colourful scraps and seated on a plywood box, *Malinche* might have been put together by survivors or successors in shaky possession of the facts. History, to Durham, is wayward, rumoured rather than dependable. In a video commissioned by ICA he can be seen exploring the deep past, in a narrative called *The East London Coelecanth*. In this a dredging of pre-history is related to a ramshackle present in which the enquirers confuse East Londons all over the

My Book, The East London Coelacanth, Sometimes Called, Troubled Waters; The Story of British Sea-Power (ICA Vook Works. £17.50)

world, and end up with something from Billingsgate on a heavy rope. And then, in 'the book of the exhibition'*, Europe's favourite myths are re-told, inflected by Native American likelihoods. The total impression, though, is of the present as provisional, as seen from another stand-point, as already a collection of sociofacts beyond recall — already passing into poetics.

JOHN McDONALD

The Turner Prize: The Uses of Philistinism

'Such is the culture we live and work in', concluded Rachel Whiteread as she accepted £20,000 for winning the 1993 Turner Prize. This wasn't a breezy *'C'est la vie'*, but a solemn, sour moan. Whiteread's *House* — a concrete cast of a house in south London — has been in the news for weeks, and is generally accepted as the reason she secured the award, even though it doesn't fit within the official guidelines. The Turner Prize is given to 'a British artist under fifty for an outstanding exhibition or other presentation of their work in the twelve months preceding 30 June'. *House* was finished in late October after three months of construction. However, the awards ceremony provided a platform for Tate director and head of the judging panel, Nicholas Serota, then the artist herself, to express their sorrow that this concrete edifice had not received a month's stay of execution. In a small way, Whiteread's work is being turned into a cause célèbre, like Richard Serra's *Titled Arc,* which was removed from New York's Federal Plaza as the result of a 1987 court case. The only difference is that Serra's work was a permanent installation whereas *House* was always agreed to be temporary.

On the night of the Turner Prize presentation, one of Channel 4's invited panel, Dan Cameron, pronounced *House* as one of Britain's 'masterworks at the end of the twentieth century'. But Bow council — deaf to the hyperbole of the experts — have decided to stick to their original demolition schedule, and are now sure to be damned as iconoclasts and philistines. The council might feel that *House* is an eyesore, but it will be said that they were threatened by the 'subversive' nature of the work, which purports to be a comment on inadequate public housing.

Such controversy is the life-blood of the Turner Prize, which, since its inception in 1984, has been the most provocative event in the British art calendar. The prize was suspended in 1990, when previous sponsors, the bond-brokers Drexel Burnham Lambert, pulled out. In 1991 Channel 4 television took over sponsorship, introducing a number of significant innovations: the prize money was raised from £10,000 to £20,000 and a short-list of four artists chosen by a panel of experts. For one month the Tate Gallery hosts a special exhibition of these artists' work, culminating in a black-tie dinner where the winner is announced. On the night, Channel 4 televises the announcement along with a documentary about the four finalists. The other three artists on this year's short-list were abstract painter, Sean Scully, photographer, Hannah Collins, and installation artist, Vong Phaophanit.

It is no secret that the new-look Turner Prize is modelled on the Booker Prize, which has made such inroads into the public imagination in recent years and helped sell some unlikely novels. Like the Booker, the judges' short-list is a subject of relentless criticism. But after three years a pattern has been formed: the controversy is boringly similar. Detractors wheel out the same anger and indignation, supporters adopt the same defensive postures and fall back on the same comfortable clichés. It is an act of pre-Christmas cartharsis, a grotesque masque in which everybody is able to congratulate themselves on their own moral purity while spitting on the pretensions of their opponents. One might imagine that playing the identical role year after year is enough to induce ennui and cynicism into the hearts of all concerned, yet the events of 1993 indicate that the opposite is happening. This year the Turner Prize was treated with such seriousness that Channel 4 allowed no dissenting voices into their coverage, while speakers launched urgent attacks on those absent critics.

Nicholas Serota said that our children will regard us as having failed them if we do not sustain our 'brightest and most creative people'. But his glowing words were outpurpled by Peter Palumbo, Chairman of the Arts Council, who castigated the 'dunces' who dared criticise the Turner Prize and the nominated artists. He compared them to the dunces who refused to recognise the genius of Inigo Jones, Christopher Wren, Henry Moore,

Cézanne, Manet, Monet, Gaugin and Turner himself. To drive home his point he chose the novel example of Vincent Van Gogh 'who, in the course of a life-time, managed to sell one painting – and that was to his brother Leo *(sic)*, the art-dealer'.

Every so often, in the midst of this windy, rhetorical hogwash Palumbo paused to await the storms of applause he knew would be forthcoming. But the tempest followed a steep down-curve. By the end, his pauses were met by the merest trickle of nervous clapping. Apparently even the Tate's Patrons of New Art were hesitant to see the four nominees as 'the Turners in our midst'.

Lord Palumbo's speech was a compendium of platitudes and myths about modern art. There was the Van Gogh syndrome – the artist as misunderstood, unappreciated genius sure to be vindicated by history; critics of the prize were 'mired in the amber of prejudice'. Art was compared to science and industry, needing 'research and development' in order to advance. He seemed to baffle his audience when he announced: 'To move forward, to expand our horizons . . . we must give the artist the right to fail.'

Not once did Palumbo part company with the central and abiding fantasy of contemporary art: the continuing vitality of an avant-garde. This idea had been dealt with most effectively, two weeks previously, by the American critic, Hilton Kramer, in a 'Turner Prize Debate' organised by the Tate. Kramer observed that the Turner Prize had generated 'an absolute storm of uninteresting controversy', and suggested that the night's discussion was meant to supply an ele-ment of drama missing in the art itself. Kramer felt that the Turner Prize selection was determined by stereotyped ideas of the avant-garde which hadn't had any substance since the early 1960s, when the Pop artists began to demolish the dividing line between high and low culture. Viewing the Turner Prize exhibition was like seeing *Waiting for Godot* for the fifteenth time: you know all the words and even the pauses. You know Godot isn't going to show up and you've got over your disappointment.

To say Kramer won the 'debate' might imply there was some kind of effective opposition. But his opponent for the night, Michael Craig-Martin of Gold-smiths College, made his speech into a 'portrait of the artist as a young Duchampian', reminding us of what an infinitely strange and complex thing is the work of art. He suggested that the avant-garde had an ongoing role to play, but he never challenged any of Kramer's arguments to the contrary.

Even more disappointing were the 'distinguished guests' invited to test out the speakers – artist John Wonnacott, and critics Sarah Kent of *Time Out* and Andrew Graham Dixon of *The Independent*. Wonnacott, an opponent of the Turner Prize, was broadly in agreement with Kramer, but Kent and Graham-Dixon – as former Turner Prize judges and promoters of new British art – might have been expected to go on the attack. Instead, they had almost nothing to say.

Kramer had been unimpressed by Vong Phaophanit's *Rice Field*, the work which had stirred up the most publicity. Kent asked if this meant he thought the artist was 'bogus'.

'You misunderstand me,' replied Kramer, 'I didn't say he was bogus. I just think it's a very *small* phenomenon. I hope you're not going to tell me that the rice is a profound statement about the political plight of South-East Asia.'

'No,' said Kent. End of question.

Perhaps the fundamental reason why no-one came up with a positive argument against Hilton Kramer was that there simply isn't a case to be made for the continuing viability of the avant-garde, except as a marketing concept. An artist may be 'new' on the scene, but it is extremely unlikely that he or she will be able to add anything new to the language of art or push back the boundaries of public taste. These boundaries have already been distended to the point of invisibility by museums, private and corporate collectors for whom the words 'quality' and 'novelty' have become synonymous. Today's avant-garde is nurtured by the institutions that once greeted new art with scorn. The artist feels obliged to act out a poor parody of rebelliousness – striking the right poses and attitudes, as though one was surrounded by enemies instead of sycophants. Rachel Whiteread's surly response on receiving the Turner Prize cheque was entirely characteristic – the artist must always be prepared to bite the hand that feeds; to show contempt for mere money, as though one's mind is set only on higher spiritual goals.

The myth of the avant-garde is a necessary fiction, an article of faith for the entire apparatus of contemporary art. The market, the museums and the media feed on the expectation that artists will keep producing works that *épater la bour-geoisie* and teach us new ways of seeing the world. The simple observation that it is the bourgeoisie who buy these works for ever higher prices, and dominate museum organisations like the Tate's Patrons of New Art, causes not the slightest flicker of scepticism. Neither does the ever-growing number of Museums of Contemporary Art in cities eager to show the rest of the world how 'progressive' they are. France is completely overrun with such art centres – all subsidised, all requiring a steady stream of product to justify their existence.

For an activity so self-consciously radical and shocking as avant-garde art, there seem to be an extraordinary number of venues in which it can be shown, and a vast amount of money invested in its well-being. In this culture, which Rachel Whiteread finds so blinkered and oppressive, the avant-garde is no more threatening (nor any less exclusive) than a London club. But to maintain the illusion of eking out a precarious existence on the front-line of art, one has to believe there is some overwhelming opposition. It is too banal to say, with Lord Palumbo, that the art critics are the progressive artist's worst enemies. Appreciative criticism is one of the main reasons why so much banal or oblique art achieves such widespread institutional support. (Rachel Whiteread is praised in the Turner Prize brochure for her 'monumentalisation of the mundane').

Writers like Brian Sewell and Giles Auty are often condemned for their hostile attitudes towards the brightest and best, but one or two villains are not enough to fill the bill. It is the entire culture which is the real opponent: the ingrained philistinism of the British public, who are ready to savage the artist and his work should the walls of institutional protection be taken away.

Such attitudes are aired with greatest frequency. For instance, in *The Independent* of 6 November, Gordon Burn and the sculptor Richard Wentworth discussed: 'what makes being modern in Britain so hopelessly difficult'; how our 'passive, collaborative culture' finds any individual action 'a gross impertinence'; how people are 'threatened when commonplace things are used in art'. It must be some consolation to Wentworth that, as he was saying this, the Serpentine Gallery was giving him a survey show. At the same time, 35-year-old Julian Opie, another of Britain's 'new' sculptors was confronting our collaborative culture with a monumental one-man show at the Hayward Gallery.

Andrew Graham-Dixon hit out at the philistines in a column in *The Independent* (24 November) noting how the (other) newspapers always greet the Turner Prize with cries of: 'But is it art?'. Graham-Dixon diagnoses that the Turner Prize does not promote 'public discussion' about contemporary art, so much as public derision. Yet he welcomes this because it shows: 'how almost primevally backward, how dull, how embarrassingly narrow-minded and ill-informed most discussion about contemporary art in this country remains. It brings the myriad dullards who don't know much about art but know what they like (it always turns out to be portraits and landscapes) creeping out of the woodwork and into the limelight – and

reveals them, resplendent in all their unutterable boringness.'

In this analysis, the Turner Prize serves a crusading function, it helps reveal the ignorance and stupidity of the general public who persistently refuse to be educated in the mandarin ways of the avant-garde. But this Olympian disdain for those dullards who prefer landscapes to fields of rice or concrete casts of houses, ignores those such as Hilton Kramer who addressed the artworks in the Turner Prize solely in terms of quality and found them lacking. The very wording of Graham-Dixon's lament reveals a predilection for novelty. Are portraits and landscapes all damned by association with the dullards? Are these genres no longer legitimate territory for contemporary artists?

It should be no surprise to anyone that questions such as 'Is it art?' are asked every year by the press. In courting maximum publicity, the organisers of the Turner Prize must expect hackneyed responses. New art has been greeted in this way for so much of the twentieth century that it scarcely warranted an aggressive denunciation. In his assault on the dullards – akin to Lord Palumbo's 'dunces' – Graham-Dixon found a much easier opponent than Hilton Kramer.

If one looks behind the veils of rhetoric, the Turner Prize is revealed as nothing better than a publicity stunt on behalf of a particular version of contemporary art. It has succeeded in attracting visitors to the Tate and stimulating comment on contemporary art. And yet it is a publicity stunt in which the leading actors are beginning to believe their own hype. Surely the greatest danger that faces the Turner Prize is public boredom and indifference, not public hostility. Rather than turning on the dunces and the dullards, the Turner Prize supporters should be grateful to them for all the extra coverage they have generated – a coverage entirely out of proportion to the intrinsic interest of the exhibited artworks.

When Lord Palumbo tells us: 'The artist is the most important member of society . . . because art, at its very best, is the highest achievement of which the human spirit is capable,' he is praising today's avant-gardists in terms that recall the high Romantic era. Many contemporary artists are intent on tearing down such lofty ideas about the human spirit. Artworks are used for crude political sloganeering or to comment, endlessly, on art's own degraded status as a commodity. Many artists are professionals rather than visionaries, obsessed with a clearly-defined task of career-building. Ultimately we arrive at those such as Gilbert and George or Jeff Koons, whose (literally) naked self-promotion; whose forays into Kitsch and pornography, are greeted with an avalanche of adulation.

One need not doubt the sincerity of the artists in the Turner Prize in observing that nothing in the exhibition seemed as novel or significant as the claims that were made for it. Yet for most contemporary artists, the criteria for selection on the short-list must seem depressingly narrow. Even though thousands of nominations are received, there is no indictation that the judges pay the slightest attention to this token gesture towards democracy.

Hannah Collins was nominated for a show in Istanbul, Rachel Whiteread for a museum exhibition in Eindhoven, Vong Phaophanit for being included in the Aperto section of the Venice Biennale, and Sean Scully for a restrospective in Fort Worth. Very few people, other than a narrow band of arts professionals, would have seen *any* of these shows. It's impossible to believe that the judges themselves would have seen them. It seems as though an artist has to be already accepted internationally, before he or she is eligible for the Prize.

The unquestioning praise of the new and the emphasis on artists who are internationally successful, seem no less a reflection of British philistinism as any of the tabloid stories that ask: 'But is it art?' Artists who live and show mainly in Britain are considered less worthy than those who have won the approval of Europeans or Americans. Even more questionable is the role assumed by the Tate, as Britain's leading museum of modern art, in actively shaping contemporary taste. The Turner Prize presents a model for the kind of art the Tate considers important – a model which can only be discouraging to more conventional painters or sculptors, or even artists who have reached the age of fifty without seeing their work enter the country's major public collection.

When museums become taste-makers they surrender even the pretence of an objectivity which they should otherwise hold sacred. When they become crusaders for the new and strike out angrily at critics, they reveal authoritarian tendencies, when they should be receptive to differences of opinion. Above all, in the way the Prize presents contemporary art, in snack-sized parcels of gimmickry and controversy, it collaborates with the dominant tendency of our age to turn · complexity into caricature for easy public consumption. This is the approved practice of the tabloids, the television (particularly self-regarding arts programmes such as *The Late Show*), and increasingly the so-called quality papers. That it does so, while simultaneously attacking the public philistinism it has done everything to encourage, seems doubly dishonest.

Photography

FERGUS ALLEN

Clothes and Grass

At about the time that the National Portrait Gallery's new Photography Gallery opened in 1993, a small exhibition called *Fashion in Photographs 1860–1940* was being shown in one of the other rooms. At this we were invited to do the all-but-impossible and ignore the faces of the subjects while concentrating on their clothes, to see how the utilitarian garb of the working classes gradually impinged on the mid-Victorian formality of the bourgeoisie and *haut monde*. Many of the pictures originated in studios with famous names like Lafayette, Bassano, Elliott & Fry, and W. & D. Downey, but some had been taken by competent amateurs. In faded sepia or black and white, they did not buttonhole the passer-by, but they rewarded the attentive viewer with an abundance of socio-logical and gossipy titbits. However, it was not an exhibition for those on the lookout for pictorial novelty or the creations of artist-photographers. Its purpose was to show us records of sartorial style and the work of the modiste.

As one made one's way from image to image, it was important to remember that this was the period before the central heating we now take for granted. The living-rooms of the middle-classes may have been well if not uniformly heated in winter, but most people most of the time had to dress for warmth. So serge and covert cloth were a frequent counterpoint to the silk and pearls of ladies *en grande tenue*. In the 'sixties, the men sat stiffly in their frock coats and cravats while their women, tightly corseted, held them at bay outside the crinoline cages that supported their billowing skirts. Meanwhile their sturdy but deferential minions, photographed from time to time outside the stables or the kitchen door by a kindly employer, made do in hopsack or rough cotton. By the 'eighties, at the beginning of the dress reform movement, the clothes of the beau monde had become a little easier and more flamboyant, though no less expensive and labour-intensive. It was a time – at least at the soirées – of bare arms and bosoms and cleavages, when one old man was heard to remark that he had seen nothing like it 'since he was weaned'. So, in her glory, we saw Belle Hilton – or Lady Dunlo, as she became after her secret and strongly opposed marriage to Viscount Dunlo, son of the Earl of Clancarty. And it was a time when each occupation or canonical hour had its appointed livery, and much of the time at house parties was spent in shifting

The Strachey Family

Trench Lines at Beaumont Hamel

from one costume to another. Mrs Freddy, a character in Elizabeth Robbins's novel *The Convert,* was said to have 'died of changing her clothes'.

But while these high jinks went on in the drawing rooms of the country houses and Belgravia, May Morris was coming up in the outside lane in pseudo-mediaeval velvet. And suddenly we find the Strachey family in 1893, all thirteen of them, in garments ranging from the slightly old-fashioned to what we would now call Edwardian. Though the men – one in a Norfolk jacket and the others in jackets without slits at the back – show signs of the times, it is amongst the women, given a greater freedom of movement, that the change is most marked. Lytton (third from the right, back to camera) would have been a leggy thirteen or fourteen at this date, and it seems that he has turned down his turn-ups, perhaps to compensate for rapid growth. And what were they all about to do? Dance? Play ring-a-ring-o'-roses?

But despite the trend to simpler, more practical and washable clothes, particularly for children, the couturiers were still in demand. Her Highness Princess Sudhira of Cooch Behar was photographed twice in 1910, exquisitely dressed, once in western style and once in eastern, with poses and facial expressions appropriate to each outfit. And in 1906 Camille Clifford, 'The Gibson Girl', was taken as an exemplar of the 'S' bend, in black, with plumed hat, full coiffure and sweeping train, corseted to push her bosom forwards and her bottom back. It is a tribute to her that she could look stunning in a style that made most women appear grotesque. In contrast we saw

Keir Hardie in 1892, at the time of his introduction to the House of Commons as the first working-class MP for the Scottish Labour Party, rather shockingly clad in what looked like homespun tweeds. And, of course, this was the time when the three-piece suit was introduced from America as the 'business suit'.

The unprecedented emergence of women in uniform during the 1914–18 war had its influence on their fashions in the 'twenties, but although Augustus John had been photographed leading 'the gypsy life' with Dorelia as early as 1909, men's clothes changed remarkably little until the 'thirties. The more relaxed attire of younger men at this time was illustrated by photographs of Auden, described as 'an untidy exhibitionist, in an unconventional combination of garments, all creased and uncared for', and of Rex Whistler, in shirt sleeves, corduroys and suède shoes. More representative of the period, perhaps, was Richard Crossman in a soft shirt, woollen tie and tweeds, visiting a working-class family in their kitchen in 1933. All in all, it was, in its low-key way, a memorable exhibition, and details that stick in the mind include Auden's pipe and Ruskin's enormous boots.

Across the river at the Imperial War Museum, there was another small but unusual exhibition, called *The Western Front Revisited.* In 1990 the photographer J. S. Cartier (French-born, but resident in New York), came up with the idea of recording the vestiges of the Western Front, and then spent two years trudging around the battlefields and trench-lines of Belgium and France with his camera and tripod. The result was a series of black-and-white photographs of fields and fairly unprepossessing countryside, supplemented by half-a-dozen portraits of surviving old soldiers, born between 1891 and 1897. The place-names, of course, made good reading: Verdun, the Somme, Thiepval Ridge, Beaumont Hamel, Lochnagar Crater, Pfelterhouse, Hartmannswillerkopf, a French command post at Berny-Rivière, Vimy Ridge and Grange Tunnel, and so on. In an observation post near Sommedieue were obscure French graffiti, eg, 'Poilus pensez á la classe . . . 35 . . . oui! mais!!!' Other pictures were of an abandoned dump of shells, a howitzer carriage nearly rusted away, some decaying boots and belts, and the ruins of a barracks at Chevert, destroyed in 1916. But the general impression was of grass – grassy fields described as former battlefields, grassy indentations said to be the lines of trenches, grassy hummocks as indicators of what had been shell-pocked ground. Show these to a sophisticated stranger – an Indonesian, perhaps, or a Paraguayan – and they would be dismissed as downright boring. And on the face of it, as photographs, they did indeed seem to set new lows for tedium. The fact that they held the attention at all, that the landscapes could be seen as having been in any way pain-full, was attributable not to their qualities as pictures, but because of what they could signify to people whose recent ancestors had been caught up, one way or another, in the madness. In other words they were small black-and-white, two-dimensional, muted representations of three-dimensional realities which

themselves stood in some sort of symbolic relationship to old photographs of the WW1 conflict in progress and to memories of the countless words written and spoken about it. For the Museum it had clearly been a project worthy of support, but perhaps the images demanded too much imaginative investment for meagre and uncertain returns, and viewers could be forgiven a degree of apathy. One was left wondering whether, to engage the interest of the public, it should not have been a literary rather than a photographic venture.

Reaching us from another part of the space-time continuum, the Dr Jekyll aspect of Robert Mapplethorpe manifested itself at Hamiltons in photographs of flowers, taken singly or in small groups, a few in colour but most in black and white, against plain backgrounds or two-tone backgrounds divided by a strong diagonal. The pictures were mainly of parrot tulips, hyacinths, lilies and orchids; and sexual symbolism always seemed close to the surface – at which, given the nature of flowers, one can hardly carp. With tumid involutions and flexed stems seen in profile, there were some strong images of natural forms, but many of the arrangements were contrived and affected, and the lack of natural springiness and organic spontaneity suggested too much deliberation. All the photographs were characterized by a superb technical finish, which was the least one could expect, given the prices that were being asked – $10,000 plus VAT for many, up to a maximum of $21,000 plus VAT for a colour picture of a single orchid.

Poetry

HERBERT LOMAS

Sharing Solitude

Dolphins by Stephen Spender (Faber. £5.99)

The poets read in youth will always have a dawnlight denied to later arrivals. It's partly the flush, or perhaps greenness, of one's own youth, but it doesn't paralyse the critical faculties. On the contrary, a master's diminishment can be only too plain.

But 'Her House' must be one of the most inspired poems Spender has written. The quiet pulse of internal alliteration – the unteachable beauty of, say, the best Wordsworth, like eating delicious food – belies the jolt to come and works like a trap.

A woman drives through picturesque scenery to the dream-house she has saved and scraped thirty years for. But, emerging from a tunnel of dense leaves into light, she finds 'No house, no friend, no car': 'Alone, dressed in a shroud', she beholds a desert of crackling thorn and blazing cactus:

> High on a sandstone cliff there stood
> Figures in shrouds hewn out of sandstone
> Who raised grave hands in salutation
> To her who, kneeling to them, prayed:
> 'Have you no nook or cranny to let me in?'
>
> And woke elate in certainty
> She shared the eternal desert, theirs.

The figures evidently allude to the Shrouds in Yeats's 'Cuchulain Comforted': the dead poets, Spender's ancestors, are raising their heads in accord with Eliot's version of 'tradition'. The words, simple, sensuous, passionate, are also austere: familiarities like 'dazzling' or 'terrible' are forced into their original meanings, as in Yeats, by the context; an archaism like 'elate' is part of that 'easy commerce of the old and the new'.

> What do I speak but dead men's words?
> What are my thoughts but dead men's minds?

Yes, but they've been more than recycled by Spender's sensibility. What does this bad dream mean? And why is she 'elate'? Is this an image of extinction, or of Hell, or of 'the world' outside Eden that was, somehow promisingly, 'all before them'? The ambiguity of a dream has no final solution: we're not given one, and we can go on looking; but 'she' evidently does not, as she supposed, want paradise, her dream-house, or even what she has: 'All she was sure was hers had vanished.' Alone, she begs to be let in, and she *shares* the 'eternal desert' of aloneness, 'theirs': paradoxically, aloneness is what we have in common, what makes us less alone.

The poem is a success of organisation, which energizes the details and couples them into new connotations: 'rocks that seemed shadows of the surf' are emblems of corpses, to put it more crudely than the poem does; the Platonic connotation of 'shadow' comes again in another poem:

> All my past life will seem one shadow
> Cast by the sun on a white stone.

The house, with its slates like 'dove feathers', its garden, and 'glints of gold' offers archetypal imagery of Paradise, in this case false.

Some of the pleasure of the poem is in its slow delivery of further suggestions — a complexity that's getting rarer in current practice. 'Room' also leaves you in a trance. Two scenes are juxtaposed: a room ablaze with children; and the darkening garden through the window. The scenic antitheses are echoed in antithetical images: fire/ice, grass and trees/bricks and roses, room now/ room then, electric/dusk; even the children's cry of 'Come in!' when they mean 'Get out!' echoes the persona's ambivalence. From 'the glow of bricks and roses' —

                   he hears,
Calling from the shrubbery, the voice
Of one long dead,
Poignant through the dark, that when she
                                              lived
He dared not answer.

The reserve makes the reader creative. The details of the present are defined: the children are playing pirates in a sloop of two chairs; but the details of the revenant in the garden are withheld, like the reason why 'he' in the room dared not answer. Something, someone, has been dredged up and everything is dark garden-atmosphere: the reader must tell himself the story of that 'voice of one long dead'.

'Letter from an Ornithologist in Antartica' is also about companionship experienced from desert solitude. This time it is icy loneliness, 'Just a bare rock attached to a crumbling glacier':

. . . And I lay snug in gloves and sweater
Happy to be alone but also happy
To think of my companions near by

Connected to me by that cable —
And that six hundred miles far north the tip
Of Tierra del Fuego has some settlers . . .

Peeking at stars through cloud-rifts, the ornithologist sees six satellites, their starry errands of good and evil making those distances (which so alarmed Pascal) human.

In 'Laughter' a dead friend is pure absence, while the speaker is a vacuum, which nature abhors — filled, though, by memory of laughter together. In another poem the vacuum may be filled at any moment with tears. In another, a student, at parting, misreads the speaker's abstraction: 'You are gone already', although the speaker is trying to memorize the moment's images, which he remembers ten years later. 'Have-Beens' have sometimes 'the feeling that they're not here at all', but rather in a timeless junkyard, along with Homeric helmets and dugouts of the Western Front.

The poet can, in fact, remember being bombed out in World War One. As the child looked through an attic skylight at the dark space seeming to say I AM (YHVH), a bomb came out of it; a soldier took him to a dugout, where he heard the soldier's heart beating through the khaki. If 'praising, that's it' is the task of the poet, Spender doesn't fail to find inspirations and, unfashionably, comforts. Evacuated to the Lake District in 1916 he's inspired as much by swords of light in the mountains, and his parents reading Wordsworth to each other, as by the maggots crawling over a dead ram's eyes and recalling the Zeppelins over London:

Rhythms I knew called Wordsworth

Spreading through mountains, vales,
To fill, I thought, the world.
'Worldsworth', I thought, this peace
Of voices intermingling –
'Worldsworth', to me, a vow.

Our 'world' is largely a verbal construct, and, in spite of the pollution of the dialect, Spender's faith in 'The Alphabet Tree' is undiminished: a Voice says:

... The entire ink-black sky
Is diamonded
With stars of great poets ...
Where the living shall read
The more living – the dead!'·

Affirmation, that's it; yet he quotes Simone Weil: 'Sin is nothing but the refusal to recognize human misery' – the epigraph to 'History and Reality', which is also about fantasy. The persona is a child-evacuee from Germany. After contemplating photographs of internees:

She felt a kind of envy for
Those who stood naked in their truth:
Where to be of her people was
To be one of those millions killed.

'She' starves herself to help identification and then, in imagination, stands among the condemned bodily. The guards turn on the gas taps–

        whereon that crowd
Breathed a great sigh of revelation –
Their life, their death – for her the real
Instant where history ground its wheel
On her with them, inside that moment
When – outside – truth was only words.

That great sigh of revelation is an affirmation few would dare to make, but, curiously, one feels Spender has the right: he could have lived it as well as said it.

Spender's positiveness is a nonconformity among modern writers (though there's a kindred, less robustly-based, unbeatableness in Lawrence). In Spender it seems to bespeak a security rare anywhere, let alone among artists. It enables him to bring to a season in Hell a morbid empathy only the hale could feel. 'Poètes Maudits', a twelve-page sequence, is a little triumph of vivid condensation: the essence of Rimbaud is here, from the boy with the torn halo, staring up at arseholes in latrines, to the gunrunner dying beautifully from the gilded cicatrice on his thigh.

Oddly, the title-poem is the only slightly dull, because obvious, poem; and the only dud was previously published in *Horizon* in 1941. In casually-rhymed couplets ('glass-and-steel flat' rhymes with 'the genes that'), 'Air Raid' rambles wordily, disdaining its metre in possible imitation of the news-reading, golf-playing lives it describes. A bomb turns the house into the famous war-time hanging bathroom, but not improved by comparison to mother-of-pearl, 'Where a mollusc, long-smashed, at one time did dwell *(sic!)*; and the obvious conclusion is spelled-out. There is definitely a good poem showing its head and trying to get out here, but it's a reminder that Spender can be uneven: when not inspired he can be awkward.

Yet, though not always, he *is* first-rate – and how different from the way he used to be. Not so vulnerable, far from *gauche*, in fact astute, worldly, the indomitable survivor among his colleagues; and yet ever-sensitive, and in flashes visionary. Neither the sun nor the earth are the centre: the universe has no centre other than the individual consciousness.

Now!
Each separate life, an 'I' (a world,
To his own self) within which meet
All that's outside: the multitudes
That make this time – and the dead past
Buried within the present – and,
Light years away, that furthest star
Proved, yet unseen; all pulsing throiugh
My living flesh to make the future.

It's an experience for him – as for the first Romantics – and the more awarely he contemplates the mystery, the more of a centre he is. This book shows him again as one of our truest poets and still wearing, lightly, not only inspiration but that other necessary periapt of the poet, intelligence.

PETER BLAND

Side Effects of Youth

Dante's Drum-kit by Douglas Dunn (Faber and Faber. £6.99)
Old Men and Comets by D. J. Enright (OUP. £6.99)
Errata by Michael Donaghy (OUP. £6.99)

The underlying theme of both *Dante's Drum-kit* and *Old Men and Comets* is one of personal mortality. Dunn is getting old, and Enright is getting older. Dunn's middle-aged voice is garrulous and philosophical; while Enright, more gently ironic, admits that 'for the old

most things are platitudes', or that 'age is a side-effect of youth'.

Dunn's is a biggish book, perhaps picking up a few too many 'concept' poems that may have been left out of earlier 'theme' collections? The tone is mostly jolly and relaxed with a lot of adjectives filling-out the rhyme-schemes. The focus tightens up when he forgets the drum-kit and various other given forms, and simply – like Klee with his drawings – takes 'the line for a walk'. Dunn is technically very good indeed and handles given forms and rhythms admirably, but it's when he goes walkabout with nothing but his own voice for company that we begin to feel an edge to his work . . . a sense, I suppose, of risk and its consequent excitement. In poems like 'Weeding a Border', 'Audenesques for 1960' and 'Australian Dream-Essay', details of a particular time and place (a sense of physical as well as mental participation) cut down on his tendency to brood about 'Life' in more general terms. Dunn has always had a sad angry feeling for the potentilities of lives that circumstances and social injustices repress; a sense of people being bred to expect too little; drunks whose 'boots break frosted tufts / With drunken crunches', or poor people in worker's cafés where there's 'that smell of coat, / Dried rain and a scowl / From a dead thought.' The lyrical anger of 'Terry Street' and 'Barbarians' is still there in patches but the study and the metronome has taken over to a fair degree in fairly lengthy 'thought poems' that dominate this new collection. But even with one foot on his soap-box Dunn has a restless bolshy intelligence that pushes interestingly against any formal tendencies to lock himself in.

'Clichés', writes Enright, '(how one used to despise them!) are coming true. The sun rises and the sun goes down. There is a season for everything; also for nothing.' I'm reminded of that lovely Snodgrass poem from 'Heart's Needle', which ends up by claiming that 'there is a gentleness survives that will outspeak and has its reasons.' Under Enright's ruffled and, at times, self-conscious grumpiness, there's a rather appealing indulgence with himself and his declining years. The irony is light but doesn't entirely hide the chill. Behind the jokes (mostly of 'the world isn't what it used to be' genre) there are glimpses of more mysterious regions. Enright calls them 'dream snatches' and drifts into prose – like a day-dreamer into sleep – in order to remember them. It's always interesting when a poet finds some way of letting the unconscious speak for itself. One minute you can be 'Nonchalantly piloting a plane. All's going perfectly. Then you realize you don't have the faintest idea of what to do next.' Perhaps even more terrifyingly you're 'Looking for a lavatory. Here's one at last. You rush in. You are on a lighted stage.' The prose-poems really let Enright's imagination – a quality closely related to his sense of the absurd – off the hook. Most of his poems here are short and a little cramped. They start off with a firm statement in the opening line, and then proceed to illustrate the point. Some, like 'GP' . . . 'Yes?' he asks, / Long suffering. 'What seems to be the trouble?' . . . should be required reading for every intern. Others like 'Shop', are just plain boring. What *is* appealing is the sense of the poet's personality coming through the poems. Most English poets seem terrified to show themselves but Enright's too old and too wise to care. You can take it or leave it. He belts his little homilies out, ending with a gag or a soft-shoe shuffle, like some jaded stand-up comic on a wet matinee in Southport. 'Lyrics,' Enright informs us, 'have had their day, or should have.' The collection drifts off into word-games, but that sense of having been in the company of some ageing poetical Max Miller, engagingly remains.

Michael Donaghy's poems *do* give new life to the lyric impulse Enright feels has had its day. From the opening poem 'Held', we are. His rich, condensed, but elegant language opens up a direct line to the feelings. Whatever their narrative disguise these are mainly love poems, moments of lonely insight or shared intimacy set against larger landscapes of time and space. Even when a landscape is described for its own sake, we know that someone's just been there, as in 'The Raindial': 'A cold rain slicks the garden path / That leads you down the over-growth / Towards the monument to Toth: / A drowned shark in a birdbath.' Several poems are 'about' real or imagined meetings between civilization (ie the white West) and various 'primitive' peoples. The best of these is 'True', concerning Lord Franklin's search for the North-west passage. An eskimo, handed a wine glass, 'appeared very much astounded that it did not melt in the heat of his hand as he entertained a notion that it was made of ice.' These poems are eager to open up new territories, to encourage new meetings. The weakest have a tendency to be self-consciously 'cool' or 'macho', but his best work has an almost post-war-American elegance of stance and language, reminding me of the pleasures of first reading people like Wilbur, Hecht, Horan, and Merwin.

STEPHEN KNIGHT

Skimming Stones

Book of Matches by Simon Armitage (Faber. £5.99)
The Fabulous Relatives by Stephen Smith (Bloodaxe. £5.95)

Book of Matches, Simon Armitage's fourth volume in five years, is more sombre than its predecessors though there is still evidence of the almost manic energy of earlier work. The title sequence, in particular, seems designed to display his buttonholing garrulity to the full: each of the thirty 'sonnets' (handled in the roguish manner of Paul Muldoon, still Armitage's major source) is a miniature self-portrait spoken in the time it takes a match to burn down. It's a *tour de force* of rhyme, half-rhyme, assonance, an elastic line and perky rhythms that all but disguises the prolixity of the phrase-making, the extending of a simple notion beyond its limit:

If I move my mouth it's mostly to smile,
or something similar,
and I should run a mile
before making trouble. Truly, it's how I am,
that way, and not one angstrom the other.

This expansiveness is purpose-built for the reading-circuit and it's almost impossible not to be charmed by poems so eager to please and so conscious of their entertainment value. (The book opens with the line 'My party piece' and ends 'There, / how does that sound?') If poems were children, Armitage's would always be at the centre of playground huddles.

There is, though, a sense in which his facility becomes a means of avoiding more troubling matter below the surface. One section of the opening sequence characterises the approach: its description of skimming stones – 'lend that stone a certain r.p.m. of spin / so it kicks, sits up at the taste of water' – is as apt a metaphor for Armitage's writing as digging is for the early work of Seamus Heaney. Even allusions to other writers ('lay / your sleeping head / against my arm or sleeve') have a depthless quality reminiscent of chunks of old films recycled in commercials.

Book of Matches does, however, contain hints that Armitage might be inclined to look deeper. The title sequence, for example, darkens as it progresses: after the banter about floppy fringes, earrings and pranks in the Chemistry lab comes a section concerning ankylosing spondylitis (a condition in which joints stiffen and set if not kept moving). It is both tender and frightening, a discomfiting collision between the light touch of the versification and the gravity of the illness. This vulnerability is also present in 'To His Lost Lover', a litany of shared moments that never happened, where the repetition of 'heart' and 'hurt' counterbalances the showier imagery:

And never almost cried,
and never once described

an attack of the heart,
or under a silk shirt

nursed in his hand her breast,
her left, like a tear of flesh

wept by the heart,
where it hurts

Unlike Simon Armitage, Stephen Smith is often unwilling to isolate the telling image. Both *Book of Matches* and *The Fabulous Relatives*, Smith's first collection, include hitchhiker poems: while Armitage's 'Hitcher' is a spare, brutal narrative in which an envious driver beats then dumps his footloose passenger, Smith's 'Hitching' is unfocused, content to accumulate attractive details that never fully cohere:

lorry-drivers ferrying industrial parts
to the wilderness, concrete bulk-heads and
                              huge water fans
to drive electricity out of the rivers.
All needed conversation to humanise long dis-
                                        tance
loneliness. They went by arterial highways,
rolling across causeways, spanning jerry-built
                                        slums.

This poem is one of many located on the fringes of societies, crumbling territories populated by misfits and transients. It's a feature of Smith's writing mirrored by the book's geographical restlessness, with poems set in Japan, Ulster, Bosnia and the North of England. With almost as much space devoted to the relatives of the collection's title, the book sits somewhere between the Harrison/Heaney generation – concerned as it is with roots

and with the family – and Smith's alienated contemporaries.

The poems' predominant techniques of studious detachment, deadpan inventories and the throwaway ending are familiar from the work of Michael Hofmann, though Smith's writing lacks a convincing emotional subtext powering it. At times, the effects of this influence amount to impersonation: in 'Bangkok Nights', tourists are 'watched for like goldfish in tanks; / language is directed at them: business- / men to seed the East with new products.' Only the wordplay on 'seed', too involved in the material to be Hofmann, gives it away as an imitation.

Occasionally, Smith kicks against the stylistic restraints, emotionally registering deaths – 'He died while I was there. I wept'; 'We cried the day he hanged himself' – and, in 'The Fly Fisherman', producing a brief but powerful elegy that might point the way ahead:

When he was dead I thought of irony that tied
                              the cancer in his gut
and played him on a line of nerves, of how
                              perspectives altered;
of how his fear swam to the surface on a hook.

Selected Books

SIMON CURTIS

Making Amends

Hardy by Martin Seymour Smith
(Bloomsbury. £25.00)

In his book on Gissing, John Halperin describes Hardy as 'one of the most selfish and unfeeling characters of his or any other age'. Does he see through Gissing's eyes? Gissing was a guest at Max Gate, and didn't enjoy himself there. Or is Halperin influenced by the 'unfeeling' Hardy depicted by Robert Gitting's 1978 biography – the Hardy who seems to have treated both of his wives meanly? A low estimation of Hardy is common still in Dorchester. My landlady there last summer, hearing I was interested in him, at once affirmed what a miserable old beggar he was; her mother knew the Max Gate postman who never got tipped, etc, etc . . . Legends die hard, and Hardy's bad luck was compounded when Gittings became his first modern 'investigative' biographer. Martin Seymour-Smith is out to make amends.

It is the fourth recent biography. There was Michael Millgate's 1982 'standard' work, qualifying some of Gittings's claims; then Frank Pinion's informative *Hardy: His Life and Friends* (1992), whose title indicates its thesis. Hardy, and the Hardys, had many friends of long standing, and entertained a lot. Emma's young niece and nephew often stayed at Max Gate.

The Clarendon annotated editions of the novels are appearing; there are the *Collected Letters* and editions of the *Notebooks,* and dozens of books on the work. Hardy 'studies' have been going like billyo; he continues to weave his spell. Seymour-Smith, forthright in his polemic, appears to underrate how widespread love for Hardy's work still is.

The happy upbringing in the Bockhampton cottage ('mud-walled', mutters Gittings); the good education at Isaac Last's Dorchester school; architectural apprenticeship at Hicks's office; William Barnes and Horace Moule; London, Weymouth, St Juliot; the falling in love with Emma Gifford – the outline is well-known. So are the relationships, from Julia Martin to Emma to Florence Henniker to Florence Dugdale. The question is interpretation.

Seymour-Smith sees an affectionate, caring Hardy. His approach is psychological, and the section analysing the course of true love between 'Tom' and Emma is generous. If Emma's fetching liveliness became eccentricity in later years, it did not preclude charity of spirit. Even, after twenty years of marriage, when 'autumn wrought division', there were reconciliations and compatibilities – as, in fact, Pinion also suggests. Seymour-Smith sees, rightly in my view, a widely-read Hardy, inwardly a very resolute man. After all, the journey from first novel to *Far from the Madding Crowd,* a notable success, by way of *Under the Greenwood Tree,* took but six years. Hardy's constant unconforming independence of mind respecting Victorian optimism and sexual Grundyism is a theme. Gittings's 'eavesdropper and voyeur' is Seymour-Smith's realistic psychologist. The pessimism and 'meliorism' is deeply meditated. Those who accuse Hardy of snobbery are accused of class-conscious condescension.

He takes a commonsense line on matters such as 'Did solicitor Gifford look down on prospective son-in-law Thomas?' (the 'low-born churl' of doubtful legend), or 'Did Jemima Hardy disapprove of Emma?' Little real evidence, he says; most families, about to be united through children marrying, feel some flurry of anxiety, then as now. In the Hardy's case, the flurry probably did not rate high on the Richter scale of such things.

Sometimes, though, Seymour-Smith's speculations head to odd suggestions as to what Florence Dugdale got up to with the Dublin surgeon Sir Thornley Stoker, brother of Bram, when she acted as companion to his wife ('relieving' him).

The partisan analysis of Emma and Hardy's love means it is Florence who becomes the villain of the piece: depressive, complaining, disloyal, out of depth as mistress of Max Gate and second wife of Hardy OM. Actually, both Millgate and Pinion point to her temperament, unfortunate health and swings of mood. Her jealous tantrum about the amateur actress Gertrude Bugler, who played Tess, is well-attested. Millgate argues the ageing Hardy was infatuated with Gertrude. A steadfast defender of Hardy's good name for the rest of her life, she is for Seymour-Smith one of the witnesses called on, like Hermann Lea, Robert Graves, Lady Jeune and T. E. Lawrence, for his advocacy of Hardy's basic human kindliness.

There is much trenchant biographical in-fighting in his long narrative. Gittings gets it in the neck, fairly enough, I think. Millgate is rather less fairly in the firing-line. Twice, when I checked (on 'Drummer Hodge' and Frank George, killed at Gallipoli), he is misread, only to be shot at.

Seymour-Smith eschews notes, yet draws appreciatively on work by recent scholars when doughtily discussing texts. Enjoying what he said of the poems, I wished for more, and more on Hardy's humour. The story is interleaved with pages on the 'Sensation Novel' (Wilkie Collins), Schopenhauer and most other issues, landscape excepted.

C. J. FOX

To The Final Station

The Sixties by Edmund Wilson. Edited by Lewis M. Dabney (Farrar, Straus & Giroux. $35)

Next year brings the centenary of Edmund Wilson's birth and, as befits a figure so forthright and central to his stormy time, conflict has already erupted among those anxious to commemorate his achievements as twentieth-century America's master littérateur. As of 1993, two full-scale biographies were being written. Quite apart from their respective projects, the author of one, Jeffrey Meyers, attacked the other aspirant, Lewis Dabney, for the latter's editorial handling of the last volume in the series of Wilson's journals, entitled *The Sixties* although covering his final years right through to 1972. In turn, Wilson's long-time publisher, Roger W. Straus, attacked the 'vitriol' of Meyers's review and suggested that his embarking on a book to compete with Dabney's 'official' Life might have been a factor in this. Meanwhile, a Wilson daughter, Rosalind Baker Wilson, voiced her dissatisfaction at Dabney's performance as successor to Leon Edel in editing the journals.

In reviewing *The Sixties* ('all the blemishes belong to the editor'), Meyers derided Dabney's annotations as scrappy and haphazard. Haphazard they certainly are and at times non-existent when sorely needed, though Dabney – unlike Edel in previous volumes of the journals – appends a glossary of the personae swarming through these 900-odd pages. Meyers also complained that Dabney did not specify what and how much he had omitted from his edition. It could be said that not enough was omitted, either here by Dabney or by Edel in the bulky volumes III and V of the six-book sequel. Both editors were faced with the problem that considerable stretches of Wilson's journals contained material subsequently published by him in various books concerning his travels or such subjects as the Iroquois and his life in upstate New York. So duplication is often in evidence and the three more cumbersome tomes might have been readily trimmed if this had been somehow reduced.

Dabney, however, does indicate what portions of his contents appeared in *Upstate* (1971) which, with *Patriotic Gore* and *The Bit Between My Teeth*, highlighted the book list accompanying Wilson's busy last years. In any case, the important consideration is that *The Sixties* – for the sense it powerfully conveys of this extraordinary man, his protean mind, his defiance of senescence and his flood of encounters with the world – easily maintains the quality of the not-always-engrossing series at its richest. As Wilson wrote of John Jay Chapman in a stirring essay of 1937, our most vivid impression

is that we have encountered a personality who does not belong in his time and place and who by contrast makes us aware of the commonness, the provinciality and the timidity of most of his contemporaries. 'Yes,' we say to ourselves in our amazement, 'people ought to be more like this!'

Well, not quite, some will say, since Wilson's approach to sex – rather like a diligent engineer's to a problem in mechanics – can seem odd by any standards. Ever assiduous in the Lord's Work, he remained sexually avid into his illness-beset seventies. And the critic who in 1929 praised the creator of Lady Chatterley for dispensing with circumlocutions and symbols in describing erotic sensations continues in this 'Last Journal, 1960–1972' to recount his practice of the sex act with a deadpan candour which even Edel found disarming.

Elsewhere in the sexual realm, Wilson would nowadays be branded homophobic (his habitual word for gays was 'pansy'). And he is particularly alert to the homosexual element in his journal accounts of the English literary world. As his hostility to developments in America intensified during the 'sixties (his homeland, he insisted, was becoming as addicted to oppressive bureaucracy and global expansionism as the Soviet Union), his suspicion of Europe, which anyway contradicted his deep attachment to European culture, virtually disappeared. But the Anglophobia of *Europe Without Baedeker* (1947) lingered on, aroused particularly by homosexuality among the Britannic highbrows. In 1964, he attends a gathering of Auden, Sir William Coldstream and others in London. One guest, Geoffrey Gorer,

kissed Auden affectionately, and I found myself almost submerged in the gelatinous medium of the London homosexual-literary world. At dinner, they talked about [David Storey's] *Radcliffe,* which they called 'the homosexual *Lady Chatterley*'. Coldstream . . . winked at me when this talk was becoming rather thick.

Wilson agrees with his Russo-German wife Elena that a certain fustiness hangs about painting in England. 'For the English, painting and sculpture are not exactly natural activities.'

Wilson is acerbic about Cyril Connolly who exhibits 'a queer mixture of lordly courtesy with boorishness and infantilism'. Connolly, he notes, wrote a burlesque involving Ian Fleming for the *London Magazine*. Fleming, impassive on its appearance, 'offered Cyril £100 for the manuscript – which Cyril had immediately accepted'. Then there is Isaiah Berlin 'so sunk in his cozy Oxford circle . . . with their prejudices, favourites and accepted canons, that it limits the free range of his mind'. That may be why, says Wilson, Berlin likes to escape to America. Other reasons, he thinks, may have brought the distinguished Jesuit philosopher Martin D'Arcy to the US, where he and Wilson met as fellow-guests at a university think-tank. The Herbert Reads tell Wilson that D'Arcy

had been demoted from headship of the English Jesuits for 'worldliness' and was apparently sent to America for penance.

Wilson was seemingly fascinated by the effortless machinations of the British Establishment. Encountering Auden in New York in 1968, he asked how it was that all London knew Day Lewis would be Poet Laureate. 'He said that if you belonged to "the family", you knew. But how? "You just know. Betjeman is too funny. Graves is too old. Day Lewis is a friend of Princess Margaret".' But Wilson, however convinced (like so many brusque North Americans) that the English were effete, devious and class-ridden, was no less unsparing towards his compatriots, friends included. And the presentation of a prize to him by an otherwise Philistine American oil conglomerate becomes here a hilarious send-up of the perennial feud between Bohemians and the Booboisie in the USA.

Earlier, at a White House banquet, the haughty author of the just-published *Patriotic Gore* is cornered by JFK who, despite Wilson's notorious tax troubles, is to award the delinquent the Medal of Freedom a year hence ('not . . . for good conduct but for literary merit'). The President asks Wilson to explain the new book's title and its conclusions about its point of focus, the American Civil War. 'I answered that I couldn't very well tell him then and there and referred him to the Introduction [one of the writer's most vehement critiques of American expansionism]. He said something about its being unusual for an author not to want to talk about his book.'

Wilson's use of Harvard in 1960 as a pre-publication sounding board for

Patriotic Gore is reflected only in cursory fashion in this journal. Much more elaborately represented are his seigneurial doings in what he deemed to be a microcosm of troubled America, Talcottville, New York. Detailed too are the trips abroad – to Israel and Canada as well as Europe – where the journal entries serve as intriguing supplements to books like the expanded *Dead Sea Scrolls* and *O Canada* and as inside slants on many a local notable. Indeed a degree of scandal is provided about sundry Canadian book people.

But *The Sixties* is engaging as well for its gossipy snapshots from the New York-Cape Cod-Boston social circuit which Wilson tirelessly explored – every night, it sometimes seems from the whirl of excursions chronicled here and featuring period glitterati ranging from Mike Nichols to Jackie Kennedy. The latter, a widow not yet appropriated by Onassis, is portrayed entering one party escorted by Tennessee Williams. 'She is more attractive than her pictures . . . She has round dark eyes that do not seem too far apart, as they do in these photographs. When we shook hands, she gave me a long interested look.' And, added the author of the libidinous *Memoirs of Hecate County*, 'I thought she had a pretty little figure.' Wilson wanted to chat but Williams monopolised her. Wilson speculated that she accepted such homosexuals because protocol prevented her from consorting with male heterosexuals. On the other hand, 'they told me at *The New Yorker* that she had been going out with Charles Addams, which seems a macabre idea'.

Increasingly plagued by heart trouble and other deathly harbingers, Wilson interperses his accounts of social indulgence, family drama and continuing literary forays (among other things his assault on Academe in the guise of the Modern Language Association) with baleful reflections on the transience of human life and attainments. The funeral in January 1967 of the writer Waldo Frank, a comrade from Depression days, makes him mindful of the common lot:

In the South Truro cemetery, full . of old gravestones. The day was terribly cold . . . I thought that the Wellfleet undertaker looked at some of us with a lecherous eye. The sky was gray, the sun a mere brighter blur. The wind froze us on that bleak hill . . . [The rabbi] read partly in Hebrew and partly in English, and the Hebrew sounded very fine. He made a little speech about Waldo . . . said that Waldo's imagination would go winging away into the future. Simple and austere on the winter hill.

MICHAEL MEYER

Outsider

Long Distance Runner. A Memoir. By Tony Richardson. (Faber. £17.50)

Tony Richardson died of Aids in 1991 at the age of sixty-three. On the day of his death his daughter Natasha found a manuscript of hitherto unsuspected memoirs in 'a dark and dusty unused cupboard where he also kept his Oscars'. She thinks he wrote it for her and her two sisters and did not intend it for publication; although completed six years previously it was uncorrected and full of omissions. 'I'm sure,' she says in her foreword, 'that having written it, he never re-read it, which was typical of him.' Richardson's friend, the director Lindsay Anderson, sums it up as 'selected memories . . . he wrote only of the things he wanted his girls – and us – to know'.

Richardson is remembered mainly for two things, his founding of the English Stage Company at the Royal Court with George Devine and of Woodfall Films with John Osborne, though in fact most of the good work by the English Stage Company apart from Osborne's plays was produced after Richardson had left for America. The other dramatists of those early years, Wesker, Nigel Dennis, Arden, N. F. Simpson, Ann Jellicoe and Michael Hastings, have not lasted well, whereas the post-Richardson period, as Anderson notes, saw the emergence of Edward Bond and David Storey and Peter Gill's discovery of the plays of D. H. Lawrence. 'The same,' Anderson adds, 'is true of the films which followed the initial success of Woodfall.' Richardson's work as a director was patchy, especially in the theatre. He was never a skilful stage director. The only three plays he really succeeded with were *Look Back in Anger, Luther* and *The Entertainer,* though he didn't do the last two impeccably, and he was hopeless with classics – I thought his *Seagull* and *Lady from the Sea* lamentable apart from Vanessa Redgrave's performances. He directed four excellent films, *A Taste of Honey, The Loneliness of the Long-Distance Runner, Tom Jones* and *The Charge of the Light Brigade* (some, though not I, would add *The Entertainer*), but did nothing comparable in his last twenty-three years, though in that time he made fourteen

films and directed well over twenty plays. He tells us that he abandoned England for America because he found the latter country 'more challenging, more fulfilling', but his work there was altogether inferior. 'There is a certain irony about Tony's enthusiasm for the United States and for things American', Anderson concludes. '. . . he remained an outsider in Hollywood as he had been here.'

But *Long Distance Runner* is a lively and intriguing book, not least the early chapters about Richardson's humble childhood and youth in a small Yorkshire town. He loved the countryside, animals and birds, had a passion for travel, and tells vividly of wanderings in Mexico and New Guinea, of his creation of gardens and rebuilding of a ruined farmhouse in France and, naturally, of the actors and writers with whom he worked, perceptive about their strengths and defects. Vivien Leigh, 'great star though she was, hated acting'. Olivier's Othello he dismisses as 'an acclaimed effeminate coon-singer'. Nicol Williamson, playing Hamlet, frequently interrupted the performance with comments and sometimes walked off the stage, notably on the first night on tour in Boston (the tour ended when he crashed his car drunk in Los Angeles and had to be hospitalised). Richardson had to cope with a lot of drunks, Tallulah Bankhead ('the most unpleasant person I've ever worked with'), Richard Burton ('hours late, unpleasant to the crew and other actors, sneering about the script'), Hugh Griffith, whom Edith Evans swatted with a parasol and Albert Finney punched on the nose, both during *Tom Jones,* and Kim Stanley and Tennessee Williams. Genet turned out to be charming and co-operative until Richardson complimented him on his professionalism, whereupon Genet walked out and was not seen again. 'If only,' commented Genet's agent, 'you'd said how hopeless he was, how casual, how irresponsible!' He tells good stories of Coward, Albee, Jagger and Robeson, and writes affectionately of his mistress Jeanne Moreau, his wife Vanessa Redgrave, Devine and Jack Nicholson.

Sometimes a less attractive side of Richardson's character surfaces. He says that Albert Finney, during the making of *Tom Jones,* 'complained, sulked and created scenes'. I worked with Finney several times and always found him wholly professional. He had not liked Richardson either as a person or as a director, and was far from being alone in this. I had two contacts with Richardson after he had directed my translation of *The Lady from the Sea* in New York with Vanessa Redgrave, a poor production rescued by her marvellous performance. I phoned to thank him and he was charming; a short while later, recognising him on the street, I introduced myself and he looked at me, in Damon Runyon's phrase, 'like I was a side dish he hadn't ordered'. Lindsay Anderson speaks of a ruthlessness in his make-up, and this emerges in an unnecessarily lengthy and detailed account of Ian Bannen's drunkenness when making a film in Egypt. Bannen did have an alcohol problem, but there was no need to itemise it with such relish. Most surprisingly, Richardson tells of various heterosexual affairs but makes no mention of his well-known bisexuality, as though this would somehow have shocked his sophisticated

daughters. In the end, America destroyed him in more senses than one.

DIGBY DURRANT

Hall of Fame

The Autobiography of Peter Hall: Making an Exhibition of Myself (Sinclair-Stevenson. £20.00)

This is a Mount Everest of a book. From a Suffolk base camp as an only child early hardened to a world of tin baths and outside lavatories, cossetted by a clutch of aunts and uncles, protected by parents whose determination to contrive a good education for him on a stationmaster's pay is matched only by his thirst to absorb it, Peter Hall starts his steep ascent. He reaches the Perse school with a scholarship and Cambridge with an exhibition, where his interest in the theatre is fanned into an obsession which would have cost him his degree but for the indulgence of an exceptional tutor who guided him to a decent result. At twenty-four he's director of the Arts Theatre. The Royal Shakespeare follows, then the National where the going gets harder as the Left abuse him for being an elitist while the Right vilify him as a snake-in-the-grass Marxist. Even so he directs plays by Pinter, Tennessee Williams, Beckett, Chekov, Ibsen . . . I think we'd better stop there. Even this much abbreviated list of Hall's successes reminds us that a chronicle of unstoppable achievement is at best too rich in detail or at worst too self-congratulatory to make an interesting book. There has to be something more if we are not to lapse into fidgety, bug-eyed spectators of events that no longer interest us.

Is there? Hall has made plenty of enemies, been subject to fits of suicidal depression since the age of ten and has narrowly survived the ups and downs of four marriages. Surely this is enough to give this egocentric monster, as some see him, the colourful trappings of fallibility and touch our sympathies? Hall is frank about his enemies but says he often forgets who they are which is either engaging or arrogant of him. I'm sure he won't forget Rees-Mogg, the conscience of us all, who attacked him for making a personal fortune by exploiting productions financed by public subsidies and taking them into the commercial theatre. The charge has stuck because it is true, but Hall was only following a common practice, he insists, and one that benefited many besides himself. His crime was to do it on a more spectacular scale.

Mrs Thatcher was no fan either, complaining that the four letter words spoken by Mozart in Schaeffer's *Amadeus* were disgusting and untrue. Hall sent her a copy of some of Mozart's letters. She didn't respond and later asked her Arts Minister when 'we' were going to stop giving money to awful people like Hall. Perhaps his opinion at the time of her replacement of Heath as Tory leader that it meant Labour would be in power for years got back to her? Hall's predecessor at the National, Laurence Olivier, whom he saw as an old-style monarch presiding over a court awestruck by his genius and frightened by his caprice and indecive-

ness, was understandably hostile to him and Ken Tynan, his adviser, was even more so writing of him in his journal: 'He does not seem to be made of flesh and blood but of some resilient gelatinous substance like a jelly fish . . . Behind that strange face, boyishly puckered, ruefully grinning, is a voluptuous love of power.' But only a lover of power could have faced down the incessant strikes that followed the move of the National from the Old Vic to the South Bank; calmed down its Board, faced with enormous and mounting losses, and withstood the daily glare of angry publicity: Taxpayer's money! To be like Nelson at the top of his column, a target for pigeons, was Hall's description of these days.

Hall's second wife, he records in his Diaries, told him he never got close to anybody in friendship but with four wives, two of them, Leslie Caron and Maria Ewing, international stars, two other relationships he describes as almost marriages and six children, he can't have had much time for friendship. His comments can be chillingly off-hand. Stan Laurel he sees as 'a sad and anxious little Englishman' wondering whether anybody still remembers him; Buster Keaton, a dried-out drunk, 'I wish I hadn't met him. There was almost nothing to meet'; and Hitchcock after several evenings 'seemed not to approve of anything or anybody'. Sinatra and Garland awake his professional instincts and he says of their singing that it contains 'some of the truest acting of the twentieth century'. Hall was devoted to Ralph Richardson, whom he saw as a second father.

Hall's persuasive skills and gambler's

instinct stood him in good stead from the start. At twenty-five and still thought very wet behind the ears he produced the world premiere of *Waiting For Godot,* turned the actors into tramps on a whim of his own rather than a stage direction from Beckett and after a shattering first night was told to take the play off. He ran it until the weekend chancing his arm on the Sunday reviews. Hobson saved his bacon.

He'd barely arrived at the Royal Shakespeare before he was thinking it should set up a second company in London to keep Shakespeare alive there, as well as putting on new plays. He persuaded its governors to part with its available capital and by playing off the Littler brothers against each other secured a three-year lease on the Aldwych: Peter Brook was one of his directors. In his private life he showed similar determination in winning the custody of his two children from Leslie Caron, a difficult thing to do back in the 'sixties.

This is a mellow looking back at battles lost and won, an official account from a public figure, so it lacks the smell of cordite which makes his Diaries engrossing. Since he doesn't startle us, it is all too easy to nod off and echo Hall's opinion of himself, and this is disappointing. We'd hoped for some glimpses of a monster on the rampage as we would like to think he was when firing strikers back in 1979. He wasn't, of course, that kind of monster. Take a look at the two photos on the book jacket. One, a Mephistophelean figure it would be unwise to cross, the politician he once toyed with the idea of becoming. The other a smiling pussy, purring, claws sheathed, woolly capped, cigar stub in mouth. The first a face to run the National, get the curtain up come what may, the other the one to coax its Board to let him take a sabbatical away from it and direct *The Ring* at Bayreuth or whatever else he had a mind to do.

ALAN ROSS

Suburban Goings-on

Something in Linoleum by Paul Vaughan (Sinclair-Stevenson. £17.99)

Paul Vaughan's autobiographical book, which began life in this magazine, starts off by being a report on a suburban upbringing in the 1930s – an analysis of 'self-betterment' – but quickly develops into the story of a headmaster and the founding of a school. The headmaster's name was John Garrett and the school, which he founded, was Raynes Park County School. 'Garrett was out to show that the best features of a public school could be reproduced in a suburban day school' Vaughan writes, and the credentials of potential parents were closely scrutinized. Vaughan's father, an army officer in the 1914–18 war, had taken his family from Brixton to New Malden and in the process climbed from 'something in linoleum' to Secretary of the Linoleum and Floorcloth Manufacturers Association.

Garrett, apparently no great shakes as a teacher, nevertheless had what it takes to put a school on the map. Of fairly humble origin – his father was an ex-

Warrant Officer turned gents' hairdresser – Garrett reached Exeter College, Oxford, by way of a History Exhibition from Trowbridge High School. A. L. Rowse was up at the same time and both set about removing all traces of a West Country accent. Rowse wrote a poem about Garrett 'a sober exhibitioner, a barber's son, Yellow corn-coloured hair, long of leg' and continuing 'a Mother's son not one for marrying, And only I to remember him passing by.'

Garrett wasted no time in making a mark at Oxford. He soon began to talk in the manner of Maurice Bowra and he was on close enough terms with Auden for them to collaborate on an anthology, *The Poet's Tongue,* published in two volumes by Bell and Co in 1935.

One of Garrett's useful appointments at Raynes Park was that of Claude Rogers as art master. Rogers was a friend of Benjamin Britten, Basil Wright and Nevill Coghill, and between Rogers and Garrett a whole range of celebrities was induced to visit the school for one reason or another, Eliot, Spender, Day Lewis, MacNeice and Rosamond Lehmann among them. Auden contributed the school song, not one of his more stylish works:

Daily we sit down in form rooms
Inky hand to puzzled head
Reason's Light and Knowledge Power,
Man must study till he's dead.

Garrett, on one of these jolly occasions rather drunk, seized Rosamond Lehmann round the waist and cried 'Come on you great big beautiful bitch, dance with me'. Day Lewis glared at the twirling couple in jealous rage, despite Garrett's presumed homosexuality, his hostility lasting many weeks.

A late addition to the ranks of assistant masters was the novelist and poet Rex Warner, whose novella *Why Was I Killed* related to his experiences at Raynes Park. Several masters figured dismissively in the book.

War had now broken out and the school acquired a pig and a Pig Club. One of Garrett's more unfortunate acquisitions was an ex-army PT instructor who took to making the boys exercise nude, in full view of the Kingston by-pass. He was later sacked from another school for interfering with a pupil.

In 1942, by which time twenty or so Raynes Park boys had got places at Oxford or Cambridge, Garrett suddenly announced he was leaving to be Headmaster of Bristol Grammar School. After the general feeling of abandonment had subsided, school life continued, though not with either Garrett or Vaughan, who at the end of the same term proceeded to Wadham College, Oxford.

Inevitably, there is a sense of anticlimax with the departure of the star player. Garrett, who described Vaughan to his brother as a 'desiccated aesthete', made occasional appearances at Oxford to visit old pupils and lobby men of influence, but it was not the same thing.

Vaughan's spell at Oxford was brief and followed by an inactive few months in the army. His account of these activities is entertaining enough, but less out of the ordinary. Returned to Oxford after getting his ticket, Vaughan found himself one of a generation that included Kenneth Tynan, Robin Day, Tony Richardson, Kingsley Amis, Francis King, Tony

Benn and the then obscure Margaret Roberts.

The story comes to life again on Garrett's occasional reappearances. A dinner was given for him by former pupils, several hundred attending at a Putney restaurant. A kind of 'courtier-like' relationship was established with Queen Mary who duly paid a visit to Bristol Grammar. Evelyn Waugh declined to lecture but invited the boys to his nearby house. In his diary entry recording the event he began 'The Headmaster, an old queer called Garrett . . .' which description Vaughan properly finds rich, since Waugh and Garrett were contemporaries at Oxford.

Garrett, whose predecessor at Bristol went on to become Headmaster at Harrow, applied unsuccessfully for Stowe and St Paul's. Lord Montgomery, a Governor of St Paul's, reportedly turned Garrett down on the grounds that he was neither a scholar nor a gentleman.

His end was a sad one. He retired from Bristol in 1964 after a stroke, settling down in Wimbledon with a former Head Boy. A second stroke finished him off. Vaughan, after a period as a pharmaceutical salesman and medical journalist, got a job at the BBC as a presenter of science and arts programmes.

Although not an accomplished games player, unlike T. C. Worsley, Vaughan has written a book that, in its perceptions of school, army and family life, does not come off badly compared to *Flannelled Fool*. *Something in Linoleum* is often very funny but in its awareness of misfits and eccentrics, rarely at their expense. Less politically conscious than Worsley, Vaughan has mapped out an area rich in

social divisions, few of them treated before in such detail or so entertainingly. And his portrait of Garrett – and several other masters – is a memorable one.

MERVYN HORDER

Silly Gene

The Goossens – a Musical Century by Carole Rosen (Deutsch. £20.00)

This highly moral book preaches the old-fashioned sermon that if you want to be a successful musician, you have to be in love not with success but with music. The full roll-call of the long-lived family with which the book deals is: Eugene I, a Belgian Roman Catholic conductor who migrated to England in the 1870s; Eugene II, conductor; Eugene III, conductor and composer; Adolphe, French horn player, killed in World War One; Léon, oboist; Marie, the short harpist, who died in 1991 aged 97; and Sidonie, the tall harpist, who survives. All kept their own noses, or had them kept by stern parents, relentlessly on the grindstone to a point where their mastery of their chosen sphere of music unanswerably transcended that of their fellows. The present book is in good-size type with fifty pages of discography, sixty-six admirably clear photos and a full index. The genealogical tree, however, essential for steering the reader through the seven principals, their various marriages and children with their various step-parents, is not easy to follow; and the matter is important since letters from the younger generation giving a worm's eye view of their parents at the top of the tree loom quite large in the whole.

Eugene III (Sir Eugene Goossens KBE, 1893–1962), who published his own autobiography in 1951, is the centre of the book, largely because of the extent and interest of the letters he wrote back throughout life to his adored father Eugene II. Fundamentally a shy, aloof man, with a strong facial resemblance to his friends Walton and the male Sitwells, he made his name as a conductor in England, much helped by Beecham, in USA (Rochester and Cincinnati) and in Australia, where his dressy, aristocratic style went down surprisingly well, when they got to know him. Picking up an opera score just before a performance by the Carl Rosa opera company, he would often find in it the markings of both his father and his grandfather. As composer he is best known for his short Oboe Concerto (1927) written for his brother Léon; but one wonders whether that one-act opera *Judith* (1929, libretto by Arnold Bennett of all people) might not be worth another airing; a good subject anyway. (He must be the only composer in history who has gone on record declaring that he considered his music should be subsidiary to the text.)

It was in 1956 that the blow fell. On his return to Australia large envelopes in Eugene's luggage marked Bach, Beethoven and Brahms, were found by the Australian customs (tipped off by whom?) to contain smaller envelopes full of films and photos thought to be pornographic. The circumstances of the case are examined here in great detail and with the utmost charity. The 'pornographic' material was never exposed in court, and may indeed have been no worse than what today can be bought without prosecution on every urban street corner. Eugene III pleaded guilty, paid his £100 fine, and remained completely silent on the matter, even to his own family, for the rest of his life as a half-broken man. It was far too many years before Australians purged their puritanical disapproval and honoured him again for his major musical achievements in their midst – the £51 million Sydney Opera House and the reorganization of the Sydney Conservatory among them. 'Silly Gene' was the terse verdict of an Australian friend at the time, and we can be content with that, not forgetting the original overtones of the word silly: *selig,* holy, innocent, naive.

There are many odd items in the book to delight the romantic. Léon Goossens, leading his platoon over the top in the last weeks of World War One, had a bullet deflected from his heart by a silver cigarette case worn in his breast pocket, this case having been presented by Ethel Smyth to his brother Eugene III who had given it on; neither of them much liked her – she was tiresomely exacting at rehearsals of her own works – but it is to her ultimately that we owe the world's leading oboist. Léon again learned his matchless breathing technique – in and out simultaneously – from his Lancashire teacher Charles Reynolds, who originally had it from a local glassblower; should there be a glassblower on the part-time staffs of our colleges of music? And the ever resourceful Marie, for many years at the start of her career the only female member of most orchestras, found that in the absence of 'ladies' rooms' she had to devise a system for changing her clothes 'at the harp' – no futher details given.

Concerts are the stuff of the book, which is a feast for the stage-struck and those who like detail about the staggeringly haphazard processes by which large-scale orchestral concerts ever get on the boards at all, let alone with a different programme every night. They must not be put off by reading how often pieces are played without any rehearsal at all, the orchestra's performance actually improved by being kept on its toes – 'a good performance – no time to worry about it' was Marie's summing-up on one occasion. However, the author stops short of any deeper probing into the general questions of musical neurology and genetics: what the factors are, if they are determinable at all, which result in musical sensitivity and in such clusters of talent as the Bachs, the Mendelssohns and the Goossenses; why a Dvorak suddenly appears in a family of butchers, a Lortzing in the family of the hereditary hangmen of Thuringia; and so on. These things the reader is left to ponder by himself.

MICHAEL HOROVITZ

Private Bulletins

The Letters of William Burroughs 1945–1959, edited by Oliver Harris (Picador. £17.50)

Three-quarters of this first selection from Burroughs's letters were addressed to his most ardent disciple Allen Ginsberg, and most of the others to the third founder of the Beat Generation, Jack Kerouac. Burroughs in fact wrote many more to hundreds of other correspondents, including myself, early on, but the editor has restricted his range to the archive deposited at Columbia University by Ginsberg.

As with most extended series of letters (this volume runs to 512 pages), one misses seeing how their recipients actually responded to and – to a lesser degree, it seems – provoked these outpourings. Reading Burroughs's side of it is like replaying a vintage recording of his end only of a fifteen-year sequence of jokey, moody and frequently very stoned telephone conversations.

Narcotics is the common theme, with which Burroughs became preoccupied almost by chance. After majoring at Harvard 'in Eng Lit for lack of interest in any other subject', he ran with New York hustlers and dabbled in petty crime until, in the mid-1950s, he 'drifted along taking shots of junk when I could score, and ended up hooked'.

Although most of his writings are shot through with experiences and techniques catalysed by his addictions, from the late 'fifties on Burroughs tended to preach against heroin, declaring that only withdrawal brings valid enlightenment. Thus in September 1959, '. . . junk is a bad deal, a nowhere route that never leads to anything but junk'. However, as heroin and other drugs have permeated most of the preceding letters, with much hypertension about consignments (often enclosed to and fro with the missives), the collection is pretty hard going for readers uninterested in dope.

If, however, you might be curious as to what ingesting yage with the natives of the Peruvian jungle is like, this book probably contains the most graphic first-hand accounts available in English: 'About six Indians and myself sat around drinking Ayahuasca as they call it, no-one making any sort of noise. At first a feeling of serene wisdom made me quite content to sit there indefinitely. What followed was like possession by a *blue spirit.* Blue purple . . . like Easter Island or Maori designs, a blue substance throughout my body, and an archaic grinning face. At the same time a tremendous sexual charge – but shortly I felt my jaws clamping tight, and convulsive tremors in arms and legs, and thought it prudent to take phenobarbitol and codeine.'

The main perks of this edition are sporadic premonitions of the casually corruscating, witty literary voice to come: 'I lost my Texas license for driving while drunk and public indecency – caught *in flagrante* in parked car. Find things very uncool in Texas.' But the effusive responses of Will Self, who has called the book Burroughs's 'best work of all', or Peter Conrad's view of it as 'his masterpiece', strike me as way off-beam. Burroughs's vocation as a self-reliant artist and writer remained embryonic until some time after he'd dashed off these fundamentally random and expressly private bulletins from his 'wilderness years' as a bohemian dilettante.

Michael Horovitz is the editor of Children of Albion *and* Grandchildren of Albion *(New Departures £9.99).*

IAN WHITCOMB

Reading About Penises

The Penguin Book of Gay Short Stories edited by David Leavitt and Mark Mitchell (Viking. £15.99)

Gay's the word nowadays. Another No-Go barrier has been crashed and those who once were but buggers, quiet or noisy, have been corralled into the ghetto of a new genre: gay writing. Quite respectable, very fashionable. Only the poor paedophiles lie, like lepers, way out beyond the pale. Armistead Maupin's *Tales of the City* is a sprawling, exulting Channel Four mini-series; soap operas and sit-coms race to produce in-house gays; even *The Archers,* so we're told, will reveal that one of their rurals may be 'just so'. Only the ubiquitous Stephen Fry can't quite decide upon which side of the fence he'll sit.

Meanwhile, as always, the meat of the matter – male anatomy and its manipulation – waits for the handling in a million shops all over the world: glossy mags and books for the down-in-the-depths market, promising business as usual: single-handed tales of 'chain gang chickens', 'come hungry cruisers' and 'brute woodsmen'.

Thus had it always been. In the shadows, and exciting. But through the broken barrier there marched, in the 1970s, the cause-criers and screamers into a supposed battleground. Yet the enemy, their fellow writers, put up no fight. After all, for years Herr Issyvoo preferred to greet you with 'I'm queer, you know!', like a bushy-eyebrowed Just William looking for trouble, and nobody really cared. The question was always: is the writing any good? Does 'Coming Out' improve your work? Like the word-processor which is supposed to make every man a Dickens. For my money *The Berlin Stories* are magical while *Christopher And His Kind* is a route march.

The truth is there's no literary enemy waiting to pounce on these strutting, sashaying Soldiers of the Queans — there's only Mother Nature, felling the Warriors after they suffer one too many deadly bolts.

Gay's the word, and more's the pity. Time was when the word was a sweet thing evoking bright and sunny meadows, Cecily Courtneidge and Jack Hulbert trolling about, Celia Johnson describing a happy day's brief encounter with Trevor Howard, and that gay old time we had at the tennis club dance when the band played the fresh-off-the-boat score of *My Fair Lady*. Gone, all gone! A dear word destroyed.

Gay is a movement, a group advancing with deadly seriousness. No jokes please, unless you're a member. No limericks about pansies who hail from Khartoum taking lesbians up to their room. Gay is a life-style. But what is that life? No more the set menu of basket-bulging hedonists on Fire Island beaches, of popper-hazed bath-house back rooms where shadows take it up to the hilt, of infernal disco boom beats, of glory holes and the legendary Human Urinal (see Stephen Greco's 'Good With Words' in the above

book). No more the Earl's Court cry of 'Let's go cottaging!'.

Safe Gay is now all style – the tasteful curtains, the hot canapés to die for, the right cut of the trouser, the ribbon on the jacket, the Streisand concert, the Midler movie. Still, at base the cruel, insatiable appetite remains, a quivering sensuality lusting for chocolate creams or body parts.

And so, safely, to this great black slab of a book – 650 pages of small print and mostly jolly readable. I couldn't put it down, but when I did I had to turn it over because of the latin cover boys beach-embracing (a Herbert List art photo). Six hundred and fifty pages of *writing* – for much of the best stuff isn't homosexual. Not 'Sally Bowles', not D. H. Lawrence's beautiful 'Poem of Friendship', not Sherwood Anderson's song of 'Hands'. Nor are some of the writers gay: Graham Greene, William Trevor, Barbara Pym, Edna O'Brien. I was half-expecting G. K. Chesterton to suddenly put in an appearance, arm in arm with Hilaire, rolling down an English lane, heading for a snug pub and some brotherly beer-swilling.

Certainly there are gay characters, funny and sad and sometimes mere excrement (the American writers are best at this). But as to being a book of gay *short stories* – this is a misnomer: John Cheever's 'story' is an extract from *Falconer,* J. R. Ackerley's from *My Father and Myself,* Barbara Pym's from *A Glass of Blessings*. Not short stories – and I suspect, not really fiction. Most of the writing sounds anecdotal documentary, even confessional. As far as decent, plain, good writing goes the British lead hands down. The real shiner is Noel Coward's diary-story 'Me and the Girls'.

Georgie Banks, chatty and cheery and terribly camp, has spent years chaperoning the girls of a third-rate revue – 'flouncing about all over the globe, dear', says Georgie from his death bed in a foreign hospital run by nuns. But there's a Dr Pierre who's 'quite a dish really he is'. Georgie 'could go for him in a big way if I was well enough, but I'm not and that's that'. A touching toughness about this old queen, an elegant stork sliding across the wafer-thin ice of his life, never quite knowing what it's all about, but having no regrets. The girls are kind and judge his queerness to be something he caught, like a bad habit. 'Would you mind!'. No, he's not done badly, far from it. Even if he's never quite 'made the grade'. But laughs! I tell you: the early years as a kid actor playing elves and gnomes in acts two and three. 'Some of us have remained fairies to this day.' And the composer pinching their bottoms. And 'the jovial wet-handed clergymen queueing up outside the stage-door to take us out to tea and stroke our knees under the table'. As an adult Georgie has his share of 'fun and games' but after Bunny he meets Harry-boy and for a brief spell he enjoys real domestic love. The partnership is perfect, Georgie keeping house in their Swiss Cottage maisonette, proud of the new set of loose covers for the divan bed, and Harry-boy tinkering with his motor bike, the one that soon kills him. 'He loved me true did Harry-boy and I loved him true, and if the happiness we gave each other was wicked and wrong in the eyes of the Law and the Church and God Almighty, then (they)

can go dig a hole and fall down it.'

The night before Georgie dies Harry-boy materializes at the end of the hospital bed – 'Wearing his blue dungarees and holding up a pair of diabolical old socks which he wanted me to wash out for him.' Clearly The Master has the touch. This is both funny and moving, a miniature masterpiece, and fulfills the book's press blurb about 'illuminating the experience of love between men'.

For the rest, we have D. H. Lawrence describing in intoxicating poetic-prose a perfect moment of love: his farm boy pal rubs and hugs him after a naked swim. 'Life was full of glamour for us both.' Graham Greene, a dirty old man in the South of France, watches two interior decorators score the bridegroom while Graham has to pant unrequited for the bride. William Trevor's 'Torridge' tells the familiar story of how public school hearties can satisfy their pashes with their bijous and then get married and go all hetero with swarms of kiddies. I thought it a bit off of weedy Torridge, the school drip, to turn up at the reunion as a poof with a cupboard full of skeletons to rattle. It's not on – not in front of the wives. After all, everybody with the right equipment had a fling or two at boarding school.

E. M. Forster and John Cheever are indulging in fantasies. Forster is Sir Richard, guesting in a country house and spying a likely lad bringing in the milk. Next morning, bright and early, Sir Richard is in the garden watching the boy unzip his shirt. 'Much slid into view.' In a trice they're where the fern is highest and having a moment's pleasure. 'You all right?' asks the lad. John Cheever, taking time out from suburban family life, fantasizes about the Valley, a prison urinal trough into which the tough wank all night. The 'fusillade' from the pumpers inspires him to consider the cock as 'the most critical link in our chain of survival' and from there to describe the shapes, sizes and colours of the organs aiming into the monster trough. He concludes that these machines 'represent youth, age, victory, disaster, laughter and tears'. I conclude it's all a masturbator's dream world, and should be in the back rack at the gay porno shoppe.

The bulk of the book isn't a bit funny, but nor does it have much to do with love. The AIDS stories, most notably Allen Barnett's 'The *Times* As It Knows Us', are mainly grim lists of exotic infections – cytomegalovirus, amebiasis, KS, thrush – and the drugs which might battle them – A1721, DHPG, AZT. The once-ripe Fire Islanders assist each other in the battle, making brunch, clipping articles, cleaning up puddles of excrement. There's a lot of understandable anger in the AIDS tales – after all, no sooner had the closet been opened when in stepped the Grim Reaper – but Allen Barnett philosophizes to keep a little sanity: I wanted to say that reality compels us to do the right thing if we live in the real world . . .'

A pleasure to turn from the sorrowful AIDS slough back to the good old days of pure unadulterated tossing off. Paul Bailey's 'Spunk' is a real 'Carry On Coming', a chuckling stream of schoolboy sperm, all day, all night, everywhere: 'The more extroverted boys held competitions in the lavatories to see who could produce most and who could send

it flying farthest. We were spunk-obsessed . . . in the spring of 1950. The sticky stuff had us in its thrall.' In the classroom one boy has a limitless need: 'His desk shook with him as orgasm was frantically achieved, and only subsided when he was calm again.' The dapper chemistry master, in the middle of a difficult lecture on gases, stops to let the lad complete his pleasure. 'Better now? . . . That's good.' On with the lesson.

All angles are covered in this vast book, the modern stories advocating safe sex. Paedophilia is untouched. Perhaps that will be the next gay Penguin book. In the meantime I recommend 'The Little White Bird' by J. M. Barrie (1902) in which the author spends the night with a little boy. 'Then I placed him on my knee and removed his blouse. This was a delightful experience, but I think I remained wonderfully calm until I came somewhat too suddenly to his little braces, which agitated me profoundly . . . I cannot proceed in public with the disrobing of David.'

And I think that I too have had quite enough of reading about penises for the time being.

IAN THOMSON

New Europe

Exit into History by Eva Hoffman (Heinemann. £16.99)

The dark political horses of 1994 may well be Fidel Castro and Kim II Sung of North Korea. Will these autocrats remain faithful to their communist revolutions, or succumb to change? Fidel himself has already made allowances for capitalism (Cubans are permitted to possess US dollars now). Probably it will not be long before the heirs of Lucky Luciano move into Havana with their prostitutes and protection. In Eastern Europe, sadly, the collapse of Communism has brought a material destitution sometimes worse than it ever was. National flags have been hoisted, royal crowns restored . . . but people still haggle over scrag ends of meat and the queues grow longer.

The Iron Curtain has lifted; long live capitalism. But the demise of Communism may yet provoke in us a Cold War nostalgia. Western travellers to Mitteleuropa are secretly disappointed not to find the atmosphere of shadowy fear that John Le Carré or Len Deighton described; where is the romance in all this bustle of entrepreneurial activity? In Albania we look for the surreal melancholy of mosques converted into swimming pools; in Hungary, for patrician dwellings transformed into dingy goulash eateries. Pre-*glasnost* Warsaw – grey, sinister – was rather more gratifying to the other-seeking eye. Now the entire Eastern Block (runs the unspoken complaint) is like the West and getting more so all the time.

Eva Hoffman travelled through Eastern Europe shortly after the dramatic events of 1989. Polish by birth (she emigrated to Canada in 1959), Hoffman understands the paradox of this nostalgia. 'What am I looking at, or for?' she asks herself in (the now very Western) Budapest. 'We need the tint of difference, of contrast, for perception to arise.' Hoffman is herself often dismayed when

Eastern Europeans resemble us too closely: the Warsaw wide-boy with a brisk business in computers, the heavy-metal fan from Prague in his Hawaiian T-shirt. There's a Klondike sleaziness to these characters; they jar with the landscape.

As a Polish exile, though, Hoffman is able to enter the minds and sensibilities of Eastern Europeans, particularly in her native Cracow where she is swift to question the idea that Poles are anti-semitic. (Reality is far more entangled than that.) Indeed Eva Hoffman's judgment of the many people she meets – Polish aristocrats, Bulgarian Turks, Hungarian gypsies – is never of the blunderbuss variety. She is a subtle, most sensitive writer; readers of her elegant autobiography, *Lost in Translation,* will know how keen and searching her intellect can be.

Exit into History takes us from the Baltic to the Black Sea through five different countries – Hungary, Czechoslovakia, Poland, Romania, Bulgaria. Hoffman visits the Gdańsk shipyard (birthplace of Solidarity), the site of the old Warsaw ghetto, even the forests of Transylvania. A dogged but companionable guide, she also makes a pilgrimage to Chopin's town of Zelazowa Wola when groggy from a hangover. In most countries, Hoffman encounters a great urge for forgetting – and for getting on, as though Communism had never been. In Romania, however, she finds that Ceausescu has cast a long and sinister shadow. This is the only nation among those she visited where change was accompanied by violent armed fighting. Indeed the Romanian insurrection was light years from the 'Velvet Revolution' of Czechoslovakia, the sweetest, the most gentle of them all; there was fearful bloodshed in Timisoara (a Transylvanian city associated with the sanguinary nobleman Vlad the Impaler) and bitterness against Communism sticks there like a fishbone in the throat.

Exit into History is at its perceptive best about Romania. Eva Hoffman has a marvellous eye for the otherness of this place, 'Central Europe's Central Europe, the heart of turmoil, if not of darkness'. The ancestry of most Romanians – part Greek, part Dacian, part Latin, practically Oriental – is strange and potent. Hoffman is receptive to the Dracula legends, and finds a kind of poetry in the far-gone disintegration of Bucharest. Occasionally her prose dwindles to a guide-book glibness, as in: 'After enjoying a period of autonomy during the fourteenth and fifteenth centuries, Transylvania changed hands and masters with exemplary frequency.' (The trusty Fodor's was close to hand here.) At other times, Hoffman can imprint a scene on the mind's eye in quite a startling way. Here we are in Czechoslovakia: 'At dusk, the light turns eerily magical; near the ground, under the trees of a small park, it's entirely dark; the sky, however, is a brilliant indigo blue . . . A chorus of crows rasps its loud, croaking song. On a small street, five policemen, hefty and tall, face a picket fence and proceed to piss in concert with unhurried dignity . . .' This is salty, lyrical stuff.

There are mistakes – Albania, not Bulgaria, is the real site of Shakespeare's Illyria. There are delights – the shabby bar in the Bucharest Intercontinental which is 'worthy of a bus station terminal

in a provincial part of Arkansas'. Hoffman is never so presumptuous as to draw conclusions about the direction of post-Communist Eastern Europe. After all, she was travelling there at a time of maximum confusion, when national boundaries were being redrawn and history was – still is – in the making. I liked her comparison of history to a process of double-ledger accounting, with each gain balanced by a loss. No doubt this is how we should see the momentous changes in Mitteleuropa. It has long since been dispersed, this mythical land, by the cold winds of Stalinism; the road to its restoration will be long and painful. There can be no better guide, in the meantime, to this new Europe than *Exit into History*. It is travel journalism of the first order.

DENIS HILLS

A Good Man

Journey to Livingstone: Exploration of an Imperial Myth by Timothy Holmes (Canongate Press. £17.99)

Timothy Holmes's familiarity with Africa (he lives in Zambia) gives authenticity to his account of Dr Livingstone's wanderings; and his diligent research into the explorer's written records and letters have enabled him to piece together an intriguing – and not always favourable – picture of the Victorian hero's complicated personality. What was it that drove this crusading missionary from a poor tenement home in Shuttle Row, Blantyre, to wander for years, like some mad, restless guru, through fever-ridden swamps and forest, until, as a ravaged and almost toothless old man in unbearable pain from anal bleeding (neglected piles) and foot ulcers, he staggered into a native hut to die of exhaustion? Livingstone's paramount aim had been to help abolish the horrors of the slave trade run by local African chiefs and Arab profiteers. This, he believed, could only be done by opening up communications with the natives and encouraging white settlement and Christianity. From these would develop civilisation, trade, the export of cash crops and handsome profits for English merchants and industrialists. But it was his subsequent obsession with finding the true source of the Nile that came to dominate and destroy him. He neglected his missionary work, quarrelled with his friends, was estranged from his family, and towards the end had to rely on the enemy – the Arab slave-hunters themselves – to help and protect him on his way.

'Travellers,' wrote Burton, 'like poets, are mostly an angry race.' Among those Livingstone fell out with were his companion Thomas Baines, a gifted artist; Richard Burton, whom he called a sham; his loyal friend and helper Dr Kirk, British Consul in Zanzibar; and Portuguese colonial officials. Livingstone showed his petty-mindedness when he dismissed Baines as 'a thief' and never retracted this insult. Burton he denounced as a 'racialist' – and it is true that Burton was cruelly cynical about black Africans ('debased and beer-sodden savages . . . with an apparent incapacity for improvement'). As for the Portu-guese, Livingstone was unfairly prejudiced against them; they had in fact preceded him on their own early exploratory journeys across Africa but were tainted by slave-dealing. Appropriately, for a man who loved yet was tormented by Africa, Livingstone's last triumph was due to the devotion he had inspired in his native bearers. Instead of abandoning his corpse they disembowelled and carefully dried it, slung it wrapped in sail-cloth on a pole where it could pass for a bale of trade goods, and carried it back to Zanzibar, over a thousand miles away. It was then shipped to England and on 18 April 1874 buried at a state funeral in Westminster Abbey.

Timothy Holmes has done an excellent job in painting both the virtues and faults of a man who like other Victorian adventurers was larger than life. It is surprising, however, that Holmes makes no reference to Oliver Ransford's earlier study (*David Livingstone: The Dark Interior*) which diagnoses the key to his subject's paradoxical character as manic depressive disorder, with its alternating phases of apathy and hypomania. As the reviewer, I would like to mention here that my first childhood image of 'darkest Africa' were prints of a hideous hornbill with a huge hinged beak, and an etching of Livingstone, lying on the ground, being mauled by a savage lion (his left arm was broken, and never properly set). The image is still with me. There are not many lions left today, and helicopters are never far away, but hornbills still honk like old motor-horns as they swoop over the thornbush. Livingstone's statue at Victoria Falls shows him holding a Bible, map-case and walking stick – no gun.

My African students used to tell me that Livingstone was 'a good man'. They could be cynical, though, about the civilising role of Christian missionaries. 'You gave us the Bible,' they say, 'but you stole our land.'

DAVID CRANE

Dog Child

The Dogs by Laura Thompson (Chatto & Windus. £9.99)

I was on a flight into Heathrow one night last year when from beneath a wing the dog track at Wimbledon came into view. As we began to lose height over the stadium, the lights below dimmed and only the tight oval of the track was lit. There was no need even to check my watch. It would be 9.45 exactly and the hare 'running' for the tenth race of the night. At Hackney they would be declaring the tote dividend for the 9.30. At Sunderland the dogs would be parading for the 9.50. There might also be racing at Wembley and Belle Vue, at Canterbury, Romford, Portsmouth, Peterborough, Swindon and half a dozen other venues across the country: ten or twelve races at each track, one hundred and fifty races or so in all, nine hundred dogs running, more than £1 million disappearing into the bookies' satchels in on-course bets alone — a perfectly normal night for the dogs in other words. Not Housman's or even Betjeman's England perhaps but for a moment it did not seem so bad to be coming in to Heathrow.

There will be other books on the history of this greyhound world but it is a safe bet that there will not be a better one than Laura Thompson's *Dogs*. There has always been a thin trickle of sports books that for one reason or another seem to transcend their subject, that appeal to a wider constituency than their natural readership but with the best of these this success has always been an incidental by-product of a serious and un-selfconscious passion for the thing itself. Laura Thompson's celebration of dog racing belongs to this tradition. If you have never been to a race you should still read this; if you have, though, you will know that what makes this book is not its smart journalism or solid sociology but its hopeless love of the animal. Her father was a 'dog man', she was once a 'dog child'; besides those simple facts nothing else seems to count.

The book provides a lively introduction to the economics and history of the sport but if anyone wants to understand the gut appeal of the dogs then three sections in particular bring this home. The first is a confrontation with the stuffed remains of Mick the Miller in the Natural History Museum. The second is a chapter that deals with the two greatest greyhounds of the 1980s (and perhaps of all time), Ballyregan Bob and Scurlogue Champ. The third, her evocation of the old White City. Because it seems to me that she is right about these things, right in her feelings, in her judgments, right in the language she employs in a way that validates all those parts of the book one knows nothing about: if she can put her finger on what it was that made Scurlogue like no other dog that has ever run then she can probably be trusted on Irish breeding; if she can write about the White City in a way that can make a casual outsider hear again that ludicrous fanfare of trumpets greeting the dogs' arrival I'll take her word for what life is like on the 'inside'; if she can successfully trace in Mick the Miller's prosaic form the appeal of dog racing to post-war crowds of fifty million a year then you feel safe with her as an historian of what is still Britain's second most popular sport.

This book deserves to be a real success. It is thirty or forty pages longer than it should be perhaps, and just occasionally over ripe; but against that it is funny and perceptive, moving about what it is like to own dogs, and very sobering about what too often happens to them after their short racing lives. She is good on the people and 'characters' of the sport, and on the fatuous optimism of the mug punter with his near mystical faith in numbers. She is good on the Irish, on the high street multiples, on the essential moral coarseness of the English sporting gentry, on the miseries of Ascot – easy enough targets maybe, but always a pleasure to see them hit.

But above all she is good on the dog. Towards the end of the book she quotes a passage from a fifteenth-century treatise of Edmund de Langley's on the attributes of the perfect greyhound that is so nice you half hope she has made it up herself.

The neck should be grete and longe, and bowed as a swanne's neck.
Her shuldres as a roebuck; the for leggs streght and grete ynow, and nought to hind legges; the feet straught and round as a catte, and great cleas; the bones and joyntes of the cheyne grete and hard as the chyne of an hert; the thighs great and squarred as an hare; the houghs streight, and not crompyng as an oxe . . .

Her father's idiom belongs to a different world. His dogs have legs like Linford Christie's, feet like Jimmy White's or – and could anything be more vividly damning if it's a swan you want to breed? – the neck of a Gladstone Small. Different language, different centuries, but recognisably the same dog, and unmistakably the same kind of person talking about it. And Laura Thompson makes a third. This is a book that will send readers to the dogs and there can be no sterner test of its success than that.

JOHN MELLORS

God *v.* Darwin

A Change of Climate by Hilary Mantel (Viking. £15.00)
Burning Bright by Helen Dunmore (Viking. £15.00)
Lions of the Grunewald by Aidan Higgins (Secker paperback. £8.99)
In the Land of Enki by Vilas Sarang (Seagull. Rs75)

Hilary Mantel's new novel is her sixth in less than ten years. Her first, *Every Day is Mother's Day,* was billed as 'a wickedly satisfying comedy of lust, adultery, madness, death and the Social Services'. Reviewing it for *LM* in 1985, I mentioned its 'striking originality'. Her second novel, *Vacant Possession,* a black farce, confirmed that impression. *Eight Months on Ghazzah Street* took the lid off expatriate boredom in Saudi Arabia. In *Fludd* she sharpened her wit on the supernatural. *A Plan of Greater Safety* was an historical novel which many thought should have won the Booker Prize. In the course of those novels, Hilary Mantel, like one of her characters in *Ghazzah Street,* had proved herself adept at 'getting hold of the unthinkable'.

A Change of Climate is set mainly in Norfolk in 1980, with flashbacks to South Africa, and Bechuanaland (as Botswana then was), in the 1950s. At the book's core is the way Ralph Eldred and his wife, Anna, react to an instance of 'the unthinkable' which 'split open' their lives. Ralph and Anna spend over twenty years 'doing good', enlisting the services of other do-gooders, or 'Good Souls', to look after 'Sad Cases'. In England they work for a Trust, which runs a hostel in the East End of London and does good works in Norfolk, Ralph and Anna's native county. Ralph spends his time fund-raising when he is not succouring assorted 'Sad Cases'. Anna struggles to bring up four children in a dilapidated house with few mod cons to which her husband keeps bringing 'Visitors' in need of physical and spiritual nourishment; some arrive via the London hostel and do not take kindly to the Norfolk countryside. In the late 'fifties Ralph and Anna go to South Africa to run a Mission. Shocked into protest by the oppressive régime, they are put in prison and then expelled to Bechuanaland. They go back to Norfolk after experiencing 'the unthinkable'.

In his teens Ralph had argued with his father, an orthodox Christian who put his faith in Genesis and abhorred *The Origin of Species*. His father took the part of God, Ralph stood up for Darwin. Father prevented son from embarking on a career as a geologist and Ralph was always to resent that paternal pressure. Ralph developed into a practical humanist, outwardly indeed a 'professional Christian', believing in 'the complex perfectibility of the human heart' and in society's progress 'from savagery to benevolence'. Ralph takes for granted Anna's similar beliefs but privately she worries about Ralph's naivety: 'God preserve his innocence, and protect him from the consequences'.

A Change of Climate entertains and informs, but above all it is a profoundly moral book. It shows what can happen when the goodness of good people is buffeted by an act of apparently gratuitous savagery. Can their beliefs and affections and trust survive? Can Ralph and Anna, back in Norfolk, repair each other's loss or will they grow further apart after that initial 'split'? Anna confesses that now she is 'no good at forgiving'. Ralph finds himself arguing with his children, he maintaining that once he'd believed in free will and the uniqueness of the individual but now sees only types and patterns. He reminds himself, too, that ironically it had been his intention to perform a good action that had opened the door to the unthinkable.

Hilary Mantel is stylish in the best sense of that overworked word. Her style is always to the point, functional, serving the characters, the place, the narrative. Her descriptions are both precise and evocative of mood and atmosphere. In Bechuanaland Ralph and Anna breathe 'air so dry it seemed to burn the lungs'. In

Norfolk in 1980 'the great wheatfields roll on to the horizon, denatured, over-fertile, factory-fields'. It is relevant to the way Hilary Mantel writes that Anna thinks, when her husband employs an unusual word, 'interesting how our vocabulary responds, providing us with words we have never needed before, words stacked away for us, neatly folded into our brains and there for our use'. It is a measure of the grip which *A Change of Climate* exerts that when it ends we feel deprived – deprived of the rest of the lives of the characters whose vicissitudes we have shared.

Nasty things happen in *Burning Bright,* too, but Helen Dunmore does not quite succeed in giving them the status of the awesomely unthinkable. Enid, in her eighties, is bludgeoned and left for dead by her attackers, but she recovers. Long before that, Enid's lesbian lover had been killed in a fit of jealousy by the woman Enid had supplanted. Sixteen-year-old, pretending to be nineteen, Nadine is pro-cured for Paul Parrett, a rich and power-ful Government minister, but she has not been briefed; when Paul wants her to tie him to his bed and then masturbate in front of him, Nadine refuses.

Helen Dunmore deploys a wealth of sordid material and physical detail. Paul Parrett, a GI baby brought up by an adop-tive mother, has not forgotten his un-happy childhood: chilblains and un-heated bedrooms, icy lino, 'underwear washed once a week, the black bits cut out of potatoes'. His adoptive mother had had a dislike of sex which 'extended to those who practised it and to those who were obviously the result of it', and Paul was clearly 'the product of sex which

must have been undertaken for pleasure'. Grown-up, Paul finds that 'his penis, always receptive to masturbation, does not respond to a naked female'.

In the shabby old house where Nadine lives with her Finnish lover, Kai, Enid is a sitting tenant, a nuisance to Kai and Tony, the pair of pimps who own the property. Enid cultivates the friendship of Nadine. She likes to call Nadine up-stairs when she has a bath. Nadine goes up, 'the insides of her thighs catch as she walks, sticky with Kai's semen, her body leaking with Kai, her nipples dark and swollen from his sucking'; in the bath-room she watches, fascinated, as Enid 'soaps the small pouched purses of her breasts'. Out in the street rain is needed 'to wash away the dried dog shit on the pavements'.

The settings, then, are real enough, though they emphasise to the edge of exaggeration the sleazy, dirty and cor-rupt. However, only Enid and Nadine come fully alive, Enid the survivor, Nadine the apparently street-wise, but in fact naively good-hearted, good-time girl. Kai remains a shadowy figure, his Finnishness not convincingly recognis-able, even when he and Nadine go to Finland and start living in a summer-house left empty for the winter. There, too, it is Nadine whom we see in the round, not Kai. Nadine goes swimming in one of the many lakes, and we can feel the water, 'very soft, cold, close-grained' as it draws her in, 'covering waist, breasts, shoulders . . . deep underneath her and she doesn't want to look down for fear of what she might see'. On the evi-dence of this, her second book, Helen Dunmore is a good writer on the verge of becoming a good novelist.

Aidan Higgins showed how good a novelist he was as long ago as 1966, in *Langrishe, Go Down,* but in *Lions of the Grunewald* he spoils his 'hot stew' by putting in too much artificial flavouring. The book vividly evokes Berlin at the beginning of the 1970s, the plot, such as it is, being a string of episodes, anecdotes and descriptions loosely connected with the rackety life of Dallan Weaver, an Irish writer and teacher subsidised in Berlin by 'DILDO, the Deutsche-Internationale Literatur-Dienst Organisation'. During the drinking and fornicating Weaver leaves his wife, Nancy, for his mistress, Hannelore (Lore) Schröder, visits Mallorca and Andalucia with Lore, goes back to Berlin, visits Munich, returns to England, and at the end of the book travels again to Berlin on the Mittel-Europa Express. We leave him 'on a blue evening' in which 'the early prostitutes, the early birds that catch the worms, have started parading the Kurfürstendamm'. On this last page of *Lions of the Grunewald* there are echoes of *Anna Livia Plurabelle* ('Do you hear me now?') and indeed much of the writing throughout is influenced by Joyce. Unfortunately, when Higgins relaxes there are also reminders of Donleavy on an off-day, and that is a long, long way below Joyce.

The best way to read *Lions of the Grunewald* is at speed, slowing down to enjoy the better passages of description and the livelier jokes and episodes. Weaver's host in Mallorca had known everybody (or had he?) from Borges to the Beats, and had once 'given a public poetry reading with self-seekers Ginsberg and Corso on a nudist beach outside Rome'. Weaver and Lore make love on a Spanish hillside, 'by the Moorish aqueduct above Nerja'. Afterwards, they lie, naked, listening to 'the myriad tickings and clickings that were the sound of Nature at work'. Lore thinks 'we're Hemingway characters in Spain', and Weaver thinks of Proust's *'L'amour c'est le temps et l'espace rendus sensibles au coeur'.* Back in Berlin Weaver goes to a British Council party and 'went among the German guests and put them completely at their ease by dismissing Beethoven (too loud) and Thomas Mann (too long)'. For episodes like those you can forgive Higgins for his often irritating self-indulgence.

In the Land of Enki has been translated by the author, Vilas Sarang, together with Breon Mitchell, from the Marathi in which the book was written and originally published in 1983. Vilas Sarang taught at Basra University from 1974 to 1979, just before Saddam Hussein became President. Although 'Iraq was a fairly peaceful country', he says, it was evidently a régime with a 'totalitarian repressive character . . . a comparatively small West Asian gulag'. The novel is set in that period and projects that atmosphere.

Sarang writes fluent, unaffected prose, interrupting his narrative from time to time to allow his protagonist, Pramod, to make shrewd comments on what is happening and what he sees. The descriptions of place are hauntingly effective. Pramod walks through Basra one evening: 'As the heat of the day let up, the air and light took on a peculiar softness; there were furtive breezes, and the dusty dryness of the air excited the nostrils.' 'Furtive' is the *mot juste,* suggesting as it does the disturbing rumours that are abroad.

Minor characters, as well as Pramod himself, are individuals. Maria, an Argentinian with whom Pramrod has an affair, says 'I hate the date trees. They stand up so straight, dumb and mindless. They're scarcely trees in the real sense. I mean, there's not much treeness in them.' Friends warn Pramod that even to own a typewriter is dangerous in a country where everything written is liable to censorship. In bed, 'rocking on top of Maria', Pramod looks over her head at the typewriter, where 'the keyboard looks like a demon's jaws'. Later, he tells Maria that he was shocked to hear that the Iraqi government would not allow any more foreign wives into the country; he sees Maria and others as 'a sort of species on the way to extinction'.

How closely Pramod resembles Sarang one cannot tell. He certainly makes a sympathetic protagonist in this admirably accomplished novel. Pramod is the sort of man to whom things happen, a born spectator and commentator with little aptitude for directing his own life. It seems a fitting end to the book when Pramod slumps in the back of a car with a tart, his head in her lap, crying, as she feels a maternal instinct stirring: 'She stroked him gently with her left hand while her other hand groped for the wallet in his trouser pocket.'

MARTIN ELLIOTT

Exploitations

Ghosts of Manila by James Hamilton-Paterson (Cape. £14.99)
Monkey's Uncle by Jenni Diski (Weidenfeld & Nicolson. £14.99)
Mercy of a Rude Stream Vol 1 *A Star Shines Over Mt. Morris Park* by Henry Roth (Weidenfeld & Nicolson (£14.99)

The novel-in-English has acquired another mini-school or genre, that of the novel set in the Philippines, in which desperate country a western professional – archaeologist, media-person or such – will experience those third-world horrors we get to see, usually, only at a far remove on tv. Specifically, the genre features the cutting of bodies alive or dead by surgeons or by dissectors, with concomitant detailed descriptions of limbs being severed, of brains being drained etc. William Boyd's *The Blue Afternoon* belongs in this genre; so does *Ghosts of Manila,* with a standard opening section designed to pull you in at once, in this instance with the detailed account of how a fresh corpse is boiled and flensed, drawn and quartered, and of how the bones, screwed and varnished, are reassembled for sale as skeletons to medical students. This rehearses the main theme of the book: the exploitation of Manila not only by the Old World but by Manilans as well – '... the skeleton emerges unmarked ... the loyal framework of a man who ... walked the city's streets, cracking jokes and making mistakes like getting into police patrol cars . . .' The place itself is so *corrupt* the word is insufficient; and the post-colonial mix of Anglo-Hispanic with Indian has no charm: 'unspeakable Madonnas standing in grottoes' to the background sound of Madonna's 'La Isla Bonita'. As one of the professionals, Ysabella, thinks: 'what national costume there was derived from nineteenth-century Spanish dress. What national cuisine there was merely played with Spanish and Chinese dishes.' Manila reminds this temporary expatriate of 'the grimmer parts of Milwaukee. Yes, that was it: that the faint traces of Europe had been swamped by the worst of Pepsi-colonisation.' As for the main professional, mature student Prideaux, he is attempting to write a PhD thesis that will be more than a mere assemblage of facts and will have the interest not of a good argument (which you might expect of a good thesis) but of a fictional character. Something of a Californian notion? The novel in which this notion is embodied comes out as precisely that: a documentary rendition of many Manilan facts, with some excellent absorbing observations, but with the merest smidgeon of characterisation. A straight historical-political account might have better utilised the writer's undoubted reportage skills.

In *Monkey's Uncle* Charlotte Fitzroy goes mad via well-constructed periods and, given her family circumstances, some Laingian logic. Just as Alice, in *her* fantasy, fell down small holes and moved around on the other side of the mirror, so Charlotte, in middle age, divests herself to the naked state of Eve and uproots the garden of her suburban villa. In her new lower world – which is not much appreciated by 'Charlotte-On-Top' or her son – she becomes involved with a cast of nineteenth-century authorities called Sigmund, Karl and Charles. These she meets in a Pythonesque way whilst floating out at sea with her orang-utang chum Jenny, or on picnics *à la campagne* or elsewhere. She's also involved with her naval forebear, Captain Fitzroy, who commanded *The Beagle*. Not surprisingly, she gets to hear a deal of discussion – much of which, however, is less than intellectual, given that Sigmund *et al* expound their theories in platitudes and seem less to argue than to sound-bite. Charlotte's son treats her neglectingly, rather as she treated him: as a 'sixties person concerned for the wretched and the earth she failed to maternally recognise that 'drought and depression were his own internal state of affairs'. Chapters of the book have epigraphs from Lewis Carroll, reminding us not only of his sinister absurdities but also of the fact that other people's fantasies, Charlotte's included, have a lesser interest outside Freud's case-histories.

Mercy Of A Rude Stream has at its centre a post-modernist, near-octo-genarian rheumatoid-arthritic provoked by his word-processor Ecclesias (from the Greek for 'call forth') to write his personal history to the post-Bar Mitzvah age of fourteen in New York. (It seems that word-processors not only encourage verbal dysentery but also resolve writers' blocks.) The theme of growing up in Jewish or at least immigrant districts in US conurbations – in this case in four rooms in Harlem – has of course been well supplied by a number of major talents: Bellow, Singer, Malamud, the other Roth, who have established one of the most significant genres in the American Novel. To this genre *Mercy Of A Rude Stream* adds in particular a documentary interest and an explicitness about sex in the early century that Portnoy gave us for the middle century. We learn that Ira Stigman's family paid twelve dollars a month for those four rooms, and that Ira earned five dollars a week for twenty-two hours worked part-time in a grocery store – not bad at all – also that in those days, *circa* the First World War, predatory teachers and men-in-parks had an almost open season on pubescent boys. Ira meanwhile, having no tv or videos, indulges a ferocious habit of reading books from the public library, making friends with Huckleberry, *les miserables,* the riders of the purple sage and She herself among others. And he comes to feel much affinity with the 'Oirish' who, somewhat surprisingly, he sees as yet another persecuted, populous minority in the States. With so much stress on Jewishness, even Yiddishness, it is also remarkable that so little of the book's narrative or dialogue has a Jewish quality or feel; rather, the prose reads at times like James Joyce doing Gerty Mac-Dowell pastiche in *Ulysses*: 'Below the funeral parlour, in the basement, were dining room and kitchen – and many a snack did Ira consume there, as Farley's guest . . .' Henry Roth's *Call It Sleep,* which appeared sixty years ago, related a boy's life between the ages of six and eight years; this new novel, to the age of fourteen, forms the first volume of a projected six-volume series. If each volume

is to cover more than the six years time-span of this one, we will get no further than Ira's early middle age – which means we may not get to know fictionally very much about the reasons for Henry Roth's long literary silence; but if the standard of this first volume is maintained the series will be a momentous achievement.

Contributors

EWING CAMPBELL teaches at Texas A & M University. RICHARD HINE works as a copy-writer at Time Magazine; he grew up in London but now lives in New York. MICHAEL FELD's books include *The Sabbatical Year* and a book of short stories, *Hands of the Philistines.* MICHAEL EAUDE was born in 1949 and works as a translator and language teacher in Barcelona. JOHN McDONALD, a former art critic of the Sydney Morning Herald, is working as a freelance in London. KENNETH MEYER was born in 1955 and is in the US Foreign Service, at present in Tunis. He has served in China and has a degree in Chinese Studies. MARTYN CRUCEFIX's second book of poems *On Whistler Mountain* will be published shortly by Sinclair-Stevenson. JILL DAWSON is the editor of the *Virago Book of Wicked Verse.* She won an Eric Gregory Award in 1992. CONNIE BENSLEY's new collection, *Choosing to be a Swan* will be published by Bloodaxe. JASON WILSON lectures on Spanish and Latin American poetry at London University. His *Traveller's Literary Companion to South and Central America* was published recently. STEPHEN BENSON is Headmaster of Bishop's Stortford College. CHRISTOPHER WREN is a lawyer specialising in marine insurance.